SC

1 BOOK 1 CASSETTE

7/97

VOICE
*A Dramatic New Concept
For Singing and Speaking*

VOICE

a dramatic new concept

*for singing
and speaking*

Denton Rossell Ph.D.

MAGNOLIA HOUSE PUBLISHING
SEATTLE

FIRST PRINTING

Library of Congress Cataloging in Publication Data.

Rossell, Denton.
    Voice: a dramatic new concept for singing and speaking.
    1. Singing.   2. Voice.   3. Voice culture. I. Title.
MT821.R67   1984   784.9'3   83-759

ISBN   0-913145-00-9

To
DELOREZ

Preface

When I have wanted to learn something I have always turned to books. I really wanted to learn to sing. I concentrated all my efforts to that goal, and in so doing I sought books and read everything that I could find concerning vocal development and the establishment of a technique. It took me sometime to realize that each thing I read left me more confused. I had more problems with my voice instead of fewer and eventually I came to realize that if I wanted to learn to sing I was not going to be able to do so by reading books. I also came to realize that they were being detrimental to progress and that I must entirely stop reading them. This was a strange realization for someone who had always been studiously inclined. I read things which helped me develop my golf game. I read things that were of assistance in learning to play the piano. Why was it different with voice? Why did these articles on voice fail to help me? Why did I become more and more confused?

Looking back to this early experience I now think that those articles principally failed because they tried to describe the sensations of singing. I now think that there is little likelihood that the sensations which a singer experiences can be described with any meaning to another person because there is little chance that two people may describe the experience in the same way. I think that efforts to assist another through a description of the sensations of singing almost inevitably lead to misinterpretation and consequently to greater confusion.

I remember the advice passed on by a famous Welsh tenor. He had been bothered by inconsistency in his singing. In his effort to solve this problem he made detailed analysis of that which he felt when the voice functioned well. The analysis described lines (represented by attached strings) from one part of his body to another. The visualized strings went from the chest to the ears, from the nose to the palate, from the chin to the vertebrae, and to a dozen other points. The analysis may have helped him to gain more consistency in his singing; I do not know. I do know that his analysis did not help me in my desperate efforts to use my own voice better.

From the scrapbook which I kept at that time, and which I still have, I find such statements as this, "The breath, in singing, should be felt as potential tone within the larynx." What did it mean? I had never felt anything like that. Still, I knew there were things wrong with my voice. Perhaps that was the trouble, the absence of that sensation. Here was another quotation, "The tone should float on the breath, assuming its timbre from the resonance chambers while it floats into them." It all sounded very easy, the tone floating like thistle down on a breeze, but it failed to help my singing. There were other bits of advice which seemed more specific; for example this, "Acquaint yourself with that wonderful relaxation which is so evident during the act of yawning. The throat is then open and relaxed, allowing the breath to come through unobstructed." Did we then simply blow breath through the throat? Was not the firm resistance of the vocal cords against the exhalation of breath an important factor in making tone? Perhaps I was wrong, the written word indicated that there should be no obstruction to that flow of breath. Here is still another gem preciously preserved in the scrapbook of one who was trying to learn to sing, "Impulses of relaxation are required. These impulses can be directed into a voice only through those physical sensations which are in evidence through the absence of conscious physical control." I could not understand it then and I cannot understand it now. There were other references to "breath support" and there was detailed but nebulous advice as to the manner of inhaling and exhaling. It was perplexing and useless.

There were still other books and articles which simply tried to relate the teaching of the past and possibly to recount the practices of some esteemed teacher. Perhaps he had been a good teacher but his assistance to singers was not transmitted to me through anything that was written. I am sure that good teachers of the past for the most part helped singers through their recognition of good tones and faulty tones.

Now here is that person who refuted books and articles dealing with singing, and he has written a book on singing. Why should it be more successful in helping people learn to sing than those books which failed to help him?

At the outset let me state clearly that my book will not attempt to describe the sensations of singing, *that* is for the singer himself to do. It will present my observations concerning the basic qualities of great singing. It will also include a recording which will illustrate specific sounds which in my experience have been used successfully. These exercises are ap-

9

pointed by me to guide you to the kind of sound which I associate with the great singers of the world. My book will avoid statements that are not supported by common sense; statements that are vague and obscure. It will not accept as gospel all things which have been written. Yet, this book is not presented with a desire to be iconoclastic and untraditional. Its author has no desire to be revolutionary, or to shock.

To me the human voice is a fascinating part of the world in which we live. In dealing with it I have experienced challenge, frustration, insight, the tremendous pleasure that comes from helping others, and the great human experience which comes through the communication of emotions.

With remembrances of my youthful struggles and the need which I had for help with my own voice, I have the hope that I will be able to open the mind to some new thoughts concerning the use of the voice. I have great confidence that the outline of practice demonstrated with the recording will assist those who will follow it, providing they work with a dedication to improve their voices.

Denton Rossell

Seattle 1983

A Special Note
concerning speech development

Beautiful singing represents a supreme achievement in the use of the human voice. Beautiful speech is perhaps no less an achievement. To sing with beauty and expressiveness is a matter of choice with a human being. It is certainly not a necessity of life but one of those interests which may captivate the spirit of a man, becoming only a necessity to that person who has determined to base his life upon singing skill. To speak with beauty and expressiveness, on the other hand, should be an objective of every human being. It is true that many people pass through life with voices so ineffectual that they do little more than pronounce words and make themselves heard. How greatly those people could expand their lives if they learned to use their voices more effectively. We tolerate people who offend us with their unpleasant voices or their barely understandable speech but we also punish them through denial of love and denial of the positions in life of which they dream.

A beautiful and expressive speaking voice is a magical key! Those who carry it have some realization of the power which it gives them. Those who do not have such a key often fail to realize that many wonderful doors of life could be opened if they carried it. Extraordinary speech is, of course, an obvious requirement for individuals who aspire to, or are involved in, certain occupations. But it is not only the actor, the political leader, the business executive, the salesman, who needs such skill with the voice. It is a necessity for each of us in our everyday relations if we would draw others to ourselves, if we would influence and lead them.

This is a book that can help in the development of that beautiful and effective speaking voice. However, it is directed more pointedly to the aspiring singer and that will be immediately noticeable to the person who is interested in speech development.

If speech is your interest, let me give you assurance that application of the principles set forth in the opening chapters of this book will be as helpful to you as to the singer. Let me also point out that a special discussion of the relationship of these principles to speech will be found in Chapter Seven, as well as specific exercises for the development of the spoken tone.

Contents

13

Differentiation of speech and song is sometimes difficult — The establishment of new habits — Consonants
— Vowels.

8. APPLYING THE SOUNDS
   TO SINGING . . . . Page 123
   Selection of a suitable song — Suggestions for the trans-
   ference of the natural sound to singing.

9. MAKE THOSE REGISTERS
   WORK AS ONE . . . . Page 129
   Early nineteenth century acceptance of high register in
   male voice — Register coordination is a particular necessity in the male voice — Exercises for blending the registers in the female voice — Discussion of OO vowel —Exercises for blending the registers in the male voice.

10. RESONANCE AND VOLUME . . . . Page 145
    The nature of sound waves — Factors involved in sound
    intensity — Volume in the human voice — The effect of
    breath upon the volume of tone — Control of volume
    through vocal cord action — Control of volume through
    resonance — Establishment of natural tone is the basis
    on which to build vocal shading — Control of volume
    through register coordination.

11. THE TONGUE AND
    THE HYOID BONE . . . . Page 173
    The grooved position of the tongue — Explanation of the
    grooved tongue — Action of extrinsic laryngeal muscles
    in tone production — Muscles which create movement
    or stability in the positioning of the hyoid bone — The
    role of the hyoid bone in vocal cord stretching — Proper
    tongue action is a part of natural voice production —
    Deeply ingrained and incorrect habits of the tongue
    placement block efforts to find the natural tone — Very
    few should consciously try to control the tongue action.

15

Illustrations

VOICE
A Dramatic New Concept for Singing and Speaking

1

The Voice of Nature

If there is one thing to be observed concerning the voices of adult human beings, it is INCONSISTENCY. Only one singer out of thousands sings with a tone in any way comparable to the tone produced by a great operatic singer. Dull, muffled, strident, blatant, weak, unauthoritative speaking and singing voices are a part of our everyday environment.

If there is one thing to be observed concerning the voices of animals and babies, it is CONSISTENCY. The vocal sounds of living creatures surround our lives. Bring them to your mind. They are clear, euphonious, far-carrying sounds. Listen to the song of the robin in the highest branches of the cherry tree. Stand on the shore and hear the wild clear call of the sea bird. Pause by the pasture lane and be attentive to the distant lowing of the solitary cow. Think how miraculously the happy laughter and inflected chatter of playing children come to your ears from afar. Recall those wondrous sounds of the night; the startling scream of the cat, the mellow sound of the owl, the pleasant fiddling of the cricket, and the melodious croaking of the frogs in the pond below the hill!

It is not *one* robin that lifts his voice in a clarion call of tenure and of joy! It is not **one** robin out of thousands that sings with the voice of God! It is not **one** cow from the herd that sends its horn-like tones rolling across the meadow! It is *any* robin! It is *any* cow!

Enrico Caruso sang with a divine, soul stirring voice and thousands and thousands who could not sing gathered to hear him. Why could they not also sing? The voice of Laurence Olivier has met the vocal demands of Shakespeare and the subtle inflections of Chekhov. Why do the voices of other actors limit those performers to roles requiring less voice? Why do the voices of so many speakers fail to gain or hold our attention? Why is it that every robin sings with a voice out of heaven and only one man in thousands has a voice to be justly praised? Why is it that the cry of every newborn baby is so free and clear that it may be heard at a greater distance than the dull and muffled voices of most adults?

The answer to these questions has led to a breakthrough in learning to use the voice. It has led to a means of vocal development that makes it possible for you also to develop vocal prowess, to expand your vocal horizons, to overcome the limitations which have been present in your voice.

The sound of the robin and the sound of the baby are natural sounds. Neither of these creatures has given thought to how the tone is produced, nor has either attempted to apply some disciplined skill in producing the sound. Their tones have been made with the spontaneity of natural instinct. The free emission of the robin's song allows it to be heard across an expanse of fields and trees, and a similar freedom of utterance allows the baby's voice to be heard beyond the nursery. How unfortunate it is that we rarely hear this natural freedom and clarity in the voice of an adult human being.

Why is this natural freedom and spontaneity

absent in the voices of most adults? Why is consistency a thing to be noted in the voices of animals and babies, while inconsistency is a dominant characteristic of the voices of matured men and women. Why is it that only a few in the world are capable of making sounds such as those of the great singer?

How does man differ most greatly from the other creatures of the animal world? Our bodies are basically very similar to those of other animals, but we are endowed with a mentality that is far, far superior. That mentality has made possible the great achievements of mankind. In that, it is a marvel and a blessing. Unfortunately, it can also work against our well being and create problems in the normal course of our lives. In many aspects of our living it can divert us from nature's intentions. In the use of our voices it usually leads us so far astray that a beautiful and effective voice is a rarity.

Our brain is composed of millions and millions of cells. Throughout our lives, things done, things heard, or in some way experienced are being recorded there. Sometimes the record is faint and unrecalled, sometimes it is strong and easily summoned to our consciousness. Each person in the course of life has been creating in the mind a portfolio of impressions without awareness of even doing so. Let us relate this specifically to voice.

If all impressions were filed systematically in the brain (and they are not) we might have a particular pigeonhole labeled VOICE. That compartment would be filled with a record of personal experiences in some way related to voice. To carry the illustration further, we might say that in that pigeonhole we would find scraps and bits of paper on which had been written almost illegible notes concerned with

23

little experiences related to the subject, and we might find other notes that had been typed and carefully folded, to be used for future reference. But, of course, such illustrations create false images because that marvelous brain of ours is not a pigeonholed desk and impressions left there are not categorized. However, I think that it is easily understood that during the course of life our brain has been recording remembrances of sounds heard, things said regarding voice, sensations felt while producing tone.

When we reason, when we seek to achieve, when we strive to develop a skill, we draw upon our mental record of experiences. We do this when we use the voice. Unfortunately, our minds may erect many obstacles to the natural vocal usage. Let us discuss that.

The voices of parents and early associates, correctly or incorrectly produced, are imprinted in the mind at an impressionable age. A casual or critical remark concerning your voice or the voice of another may be filed there. Remembrances and impressions such as these affect our voices. Even passages from literature could have an effect. Consider how an Elizabethan ideal of womanhood expressed in King Lear's line, "Her voice was ever soft, gentle and low, an excellent thing in woman" might cause a young girl to develop a weak and breathy voice.

When the voice is correctly produced it is easily heard and it is compelling. For that reason its sound may interfere with another's activity and that person may make his displeasure known to the person who disturbs him. The high pitched, correctly produced, clear voice of a playing child may become an irritant to a mother trying to concentrate on other things, causing her to admonish the child to be quiet, to lower the voice. The child wishes to please those who are dear to him, so the scolding is recorded in the brain and, in an effort to conform, he learns to withhold the voice; he takes from it its natural carrying power and full emission, and substitutes a dullness which has no parallel in the natural sounds which we hear about us.

It seems to me that we are having our voices driven back within ourselves during all of our lives. We often live in close proximity to others and are subjected to mockery or blunt demand for quiet. As a consequence, we develop self consciousness and timidity in the use of our voices; we fear to release them.

Our ability to reason is certainly one of our great blessings. Unfortunately, however, this reasoning can misdirect us. Deductions which seem logical may be, in fact, entirely false. Some examples of such errors of reasoning and their effect upon the voice will be discussed in later chapters.

By the time a human being reaches adulthood he has become, more often than not, greatly confused in the use of his voice. The confusion is demonstrated in the improper vocal usage which is characteristic of most people. When he consciously uses the voice, the vocal impressions stored in his brain exert their force upon the shaping of the tone. It is inevitable! If those impressions work against the natural usage, the effectiveness of the voice is impaired.

If a person is to improve his voice, the mind must be cleared of vocal obstacles. If he is to return to the natural sound with which he was endowed, and that is the only sound which will serve him effectively in vocal expression, he must gain a clear image of the tone which he is to produce. A new concept must be established. The original instinct for natural sound must be rediscovered. It seems impossible to get to the roots of confusion, therefore, confusion must be by-passed. It is the only way that he who would improve his voice will be able to put aside barriers which obstruct his efforts.

Animals engage in less complicated mental activity than men and their more simple lives are blessed by a freedom from the psychological barriers and misleading thoughts which torment and perplex human beings. When animals emit vocal sounds they follow an impulse of nature, they are not concerned with thoughts of how or how not to make the sounds; they instinctively produce them.

There are certain characteristics of quality and emission which are present in those natural vocal sounds. They are clear and resonant; they are produced with ease; and they are heard at an unusual distance. To a great extent, it is the clarity, the unobstructed emission of sound, which gives the great carrying power. Bring to mind the sounds of the robin, the lark, the wild goose, the cow, the dog, the sheep, and, if you have been one of those fortunate enough to hear the noble elk send his great birdlike call into the vastness of the mountain spaces, you will associate this clarity as a common characteristic of the natural sounds of living creatures. With this clarity of tone there is usually an accompanying resonance. Our ears tell us of the completeness and natural fullness of the quality. There is a concentrated power in these animal sounds; even very small creatures have an astonishing ability to make themselves heard. Another trait to be noted is the ease with which animals produce sound; it is an ease which allows persistent repetition without fatigue, without a faltering of the voice. Still one more characteristic, a very important one, must be mentioned: the presence of two registers. We hear it in the crowing of the rooster, the mooing of the cow, the baying of the hound. We hear it in these creatures when, either by glissando or wide adjustments of pitch, the full range of the voice is employed.

In summary, I observe that animal sounds generally exhibit these characteristics; clarity, resonance, concentrated power, ease of production, endurance, and evidence of two registers.

Are not these same characteristics associated with the voice of a great singer? Are not these features recognizable in the exceptionally fine speaking voice? There are those few who, by a commanding personality, an unusual histrionic talent, or a great artistry, may triumph to some extent over vocal deficiencies. It is not of such vocalists that I speak; it is of the singer or speaker with the truly great voice. In such a voice, the clarity, the power, the resonance are unmistakable. In addition to these, there are other characteristics. The clear projection of the voice brings reflected sound from the environment, resulting in a ringing, vibrant quality. There is a typical vibrato.[1] Acoustically speaking, there is a strong fundamental and there are prominent overtones.[2] The voice is emitted with freedom. The voice of a great singer is a flexible instru-

---

[1]Minute, almost imperceptible fluctuations of pitch which are centered about the basic pitch, and slight fluctuations in intensity, both of which are only acceptable as being a part of good quality when they are spaced at a rate of approximately six or seven per second.

[2]Wilmer T. Bartholomew, "Voice Research at Peabody Conversatory," *Bulletin of American Musicological Society,* August, 1942, p.11.

ment with a range of approximately three octaves; at least two of which are used in public performance. There is an evenness of sound; all vowels in all parts of the voice are clear and firm. All of these distinguishing features are present in the great voice, an instrument which is capable of expressing the most delicate sensitivity as well as the strongest of human emotions.

Such a voice differs greatly from that of the average vocalist. The difference is so conspicuous that the efforts of the ordinary vocalist seem in no way comparable to those of the successful singer. The voice of the usual church chorister or average vocal student is an unclear, pitifully weak, short ranged instrument which lacks resonance and is unexpressive because of its lack of resonance, compass, flexibility, and range of dynamics. If such a singer were asked to sing a solo in a large opera house with full symphony orchestra, he would be totally unable to make himself heard. The average speaker could not make his speaking voice heard in such an auditorium without the use of a public address system. Yet, if, during an operatic performance, a barking dog should somehow enter the auditorium, we would hear his voice. We could also hear a crying baby above the great volume of orchestral and vocal sound just as we are able to hear the voice of a great singer.

Why is there such a great difference between the usual voice and the voice of the distinguished singer? Why are there so few exceptional voices in the world? Is it that a great vocalist possesses some unusual physical attributes? Has he come upon some strange trick that enables him to use his voice as he does? I think the answer is NO. To me the explanation seems obvious. The person who cannot sing well is using the voice in a completely **unnatural** manner. The great singer or speaker is doing nothing more than using his voice **as nature intended.** He has been one of those fortunate few who have either reached adulthood without the hampering misunderstandings and misleading impressions which are an obstacle for the majority of people, or, through some experience he has been able to reestablish the natural image of vocal emission. He uses the voice in a natural manner. He sings or speaks with THE VOICE OF NATURE!

2

The Three Basics for Vocal Development

I feel that there are three basic essentials involved in learning to use the voice well. Here they are:

1. The vocalist must learn how his voice **sounds** to himself when it is correctly produced.
2. He must also learn how the correct production of sound **feels** to himself.
3. In addition to these two sensations he must develop each of the two registers of the voice separately and then acquire coordination between them.

The manner of learning these basics is the subject of the next eight chapters of this book. Learn them and you can use the voice well!

Singing and fine speaking involve such complicated coordination of nerve impulses, muscular responses, and mental controls that it seems impossible that the desired harmony of action could ever take place. If the student were given, at the outset of his studies, a detailed description of everything involved in the process of correctly producing a sound, and told to develop, through such knowledge, a proper coordination of the vocal mechanism, he would probably give up immediately. And, likewise, he might never have tried to walk if the coordinations of that skill had been described to him before he was allowed to take his first steps. And so it is with any skill and so it is with simply living. How extremely complicated are all activities of the human body! How miraculous it is that we breathe, and smile, and laugh! And yet, how natural these actions are to us! How easy it is to breathe and to live!

General principles are involved in the acquisition of any physical skill and each requires, through some means, the setting up of a particular movement cycle. A series of subsidiary movements are put together into a unit of response so that a complex coordination functions as one voluntary effort. After many repetitions of an activity pattern a physically skilled person is quite consistently able to duplicate his successful efforts.

An important factor in one's ability to duplicate is the remembrance of a "feel" which has been associated with the activity. Let us talk about some specific skills. An expert golfer puts together into one swing a sequence of constantly changing movement and that swing seems but a single rhythmic flow of muscular effort. When the swing has brought success, the golfer tries to remember anything that will enable him to duplicate it. Inevitably he associates a certain *feeling* with the movements and he depends on a recollection of that feeling. The feel differs with each skill and it is an experience which is completely personal to the performer. The pianist develops a feel for chords and scales and complex passages. The dancer remembers the feel of a series of steps. The typist gets a feel of his keyboard. The baseball pitcher delivers the ball with a recollection of coordinated rhythmic movement. Likewise, the vocalist associates a personal feeling with the production of a correct tone.

In developing expertness, the intelligent person uses every possible means of recalling his successful efforts. In addition to a remembrance of the feel, the person who gains adroitness often develops one or more other associations. The dancer is able to develop a visual memory of his actions by practicing before a mirror. The golfer is helped by his eyesight; he is able to observe his stance, his grip, and some aspects of his swing. The pianist is able to observe most of his physical movements. The baseball pitcher is also able to see something of his own movements and he comes partially to depend upon visual associations. In contrast to such activities as these, the vocalist finds little help from anything which he may see. However, the vocalist does not separate himself from sensual perception. He depends upon his sense of hearing, as well as his remembrance of the feeling, to guide himself in reproducing the sounds which he desires.

Here then is a resumé of an aspiring singer's first attempts to produce a desirable tone. Beginning with a motive to express himself and to produce a beautiful tone he draws on his remembrance of a kind of sound which he has heard. He tries to produce that sound which he hears in his mind. He appraises the attempt and, if he then feels that it was successful, tries to remember everything that will enable him to duplicate the effort. The sensations which he strives to remember have to do with the feeling and the sound. He depends on that remembrance of feeling and sound.

Knowledge of acoustics, psychology, music, or of the muscles employed during the making of vocal sound may be of help to the teacher, but they will not directly assist the singer or speaker in his efforts to improve the voice. He has only two important guides to correct and consistent vocal usage. They are his remembrance of the **sound** and the *feeling;* the vocal sound which he has **heard** and the sensation which he has *felt* when he has correctly produced the sound.[1]

---

[1]At least one famous singer seems to have recognized this. Grete Stueckgold, in an interview, stated that the only guide to the singer is "the way the tones sound and feel." Grete Stueckgold, "If You Were My Pupil," *Etude* (Philadelphia) Vol. 53, 1935, p.9.

3

Hearing the Tone

The inability to hear ourselves as others hear us presents one of the greatest problems in the use of the voice. This fact alone makes it imperative that the person who seeks vocal improvement have the assistance of someone who recognizes correctness in vocal tones, or, if that is not possible, accurate recordings of his own voice.

The person who lacks a distinguished voice seldom realizes that the beautiful tones of a great singer are not beautiful to the singer himself.

The desire of an aspiring singer to make a tone which is beautiful to others usually leads him to try to make a tone which is beautiful to himself. It is an error, and it is an example of reasoning that has led to a false deduction. The reasoning may have been something like this: Signor Alfani is a famous and great singer; he has a beautiful mellow voice; I desire to be a famous and great singer, therefore, I must make a tone which sounds beautiful and mellow. Thus far, the deduction seems correct, but the singer then goes on to try to imitate the kind of tone which he has heard Signor Alfani produce and to judge the results with his own ears. He tries to make a tone which sounds beautiful to himself, not realizing that Signor Alfani does not describe as beautiful the sound which he himself has produced.

Great singers have become so accustomed to the

sound of their own voices that they unquestioningly accept it. However, they are likely to admit, if requested to make an analysis of the quality which they hear, that it is not beautiful, only coarse and penetrating.

The reason for this deception is not difficult to find; it is only so close to us that we overlook it. Let us consider the reason. Great voices are also loud voices. This certainly does not mean that all loud voices are great. However, it is a simple fact that the voices of great singers are much louder than average voices.[1] Remember that singers each summer perform operas with a symphony orchestra of more than one hundred players in the open air in the Roman Arena of Verona, Italy, and those singers are heard without amplification by an audience of approximately twenty thousand. Try to imagine how such voices would sound at a distance of two feet. Imagine any of those singers singing directly into your ears. It should not be difficult for you to understand that their voices would sound much too penetrating. You would hear none of the soft roundness which you associate with these voices from having heard them in auditoriums or on recordings. You would notice the pointed quality, the brilliance of their voices, and you would probably be aware of the sound associated with nasal resonance. You would surely be impressed by the power and security of their clear voices, but very likely you would be bothered by a roughness which you had not previously heard in their tones.

---

[1]For two hundred years violin makers have been seeking to learn the secret of the extraordinary resonance and fine quality of the seventeenth and eighteenth century violins fashioned by Stradivarius, Amati, Guarnerius and other great craftsmen of Cremona. One thing which has been noted is that those violins are more voluminous than inferior instruments.

Why would they sound different to you at this proximity? Why would the clear brilliance and the rough resonance of their voices predominate? Why would you not hear the mellow quality that you have associated with these successful singers? It is simply a matter of distance; you had not previously heard these singers at such nearness.

Distance plays a great part in mellowing the tone; it better enables us to hear a balance in the overtones which produce quality. If we but recall some of our own experiences, we realize that this is true. Those who have heard the shocking blast of a steamboat whistle while standing close to the ship's funnel may recall the rich warmth of the sound when it is heard from across the harbor. Those who have been startled by the shrill whistle of a nearby locomotive may have also heard the lonesome, mellow sound of a train whistle in a distant mountain canyon.

Instrumentalists seem to sense this fact when singers do not. Every orchestral conductor knows that it is more difficult for him to hear balance in his orchestra than it is for the audience sitting in the balcony. Every great violinist knows that his tone sounds rougher to himself than to his listener. A fine instructor of flute playing seemed to understand the principle when he advised his students to make the tone sound coarse to themselves, in order that they might come to find the richest quality of their delicate instrument. Yet singers expect the tone to sound well to themselves!

Surely it is unnecessary to give further explanation as to why the tone which has brought success to singers does not sound well to themselves. Certainly it is now unnecessary to tell you that the tone may sound very different to you if you sing correctly. Has it

37

not already occurred to you that Birgit Nilsson's voice
at a distance of two feet would be farther from your
ears than is your own voice? If your voice is to have
the resonance which we associate with great voices, how
can it sound well to you? Are you not actually singing
into your own ears? Unfortunately, you will never be
able to hear yourself as others hear you. You can
never walk away and listen to yourself from a distance. You can obtain a tonal reflection of the sound
of your voice by hearing it recorded, although even a
good recording may deceive you in the measurement
of power, since a recorder can thrust a voice into the
distance or bring it close at hand by the slight turning
of a knob. Dorothy Caruso, in the biography of her
famous husband, referred to the great singer's inability to hear the lovely quality of his voice when he
sang: "he only felt something inside when the notes
came out well. Only by listening to his records could
he hear what others heard. 'That is good, it is a
beautiful voice,' he would say in astonishment."[2]

How important it is that all singers and teachers
fully understand this simple and obvious fact! Students of voice must understand it from the beginning, but few have ever given thought to the phenomenon or had it called to their attention. Students, who
for years have been trying unsuccessfully to learn to
sing, express surprise when it is explained to them.
How much time has been wasted! Far more than
ninety percent of student singers are avoiding the
natural vocal quality with which they have been
blessed. They are avoiding it because they fear it.
They have eliminated the true resonance from their

---

[2]Dorothy Caruso, *Enrico Caruso, His Life and Death* (New
York; Simon Schuster, 1945), p.73.

voices because they thought it was coarseness. They are making the tone more pleasant to themselves by muffling it in their throats or by merely singing softly. An explanation of this overlooked fact and a recording of the singer's voice may quickly point to a mistake which the singer has been making for years.

At this point it might occur to the singer that he can correct all vocal ailments and become the possessor of a beautiful voice by merely making tones which do not sound well to himself. Unfortunately this is not the case. An improper brilliance can rob the tone of everything that resembles quality. There is a particular kind of tone which the singer must produce. When that tone is found it seems impossible to make the sound so brilliant that it will become unpleasant to those who love and understand great voices.

When the tone is correctly produced the singer feels a complete release of the sound. Although a certain amount of physical effort has been involved, the producer of the tone is usually impressed by the ease with which it is accomplished. There seems to be no strain. The ringing quality is so pronounced that it is heard all about; to some it seems actually detached from themselves.

The singer's description of the tone and his sensations in producing it are entirely personal and vary from individual to individual. However, if he has previously only sung with a soft or dull tone, he is almost certain to associate extreme brilliance with the correct tone and may perhaps be disturbed by a feeling of nasality, brittleness, or seeming harshness. Given assurance that he may expect to hear an unusual, and perhaps unpleasant sound, the singer must dare to try. His results must then be appraised by one who is trained to recognize the correct sound, or, in the absence of such a person, the tone must be recorded and judged by the singer himself.

The successful singer, the one who has already become acquainted with the correct sound of his own voice, should also from time to time remind himself that he cannot listen to himself and hear the quality which others hear in his voice. Any attempts to listen to his own voice in this manner, to impart quality to the tone, are likely to result in his losing the clarity which has made his voice distinctive. If this clarity is lost, if the tone commences to feel richer and mellower to the singer, he is heading toward vocal difficulties.

The teacher of singing must remember that his task is somewhat comparable to that of a painter who works near to his canvas, but desires an effect which will be observed at a greater distance. Like the painter, the singing instructor may be misled by texture that seems rough. Like him, the teacher may become too occupied with delicate detail and lose sight of that which will give the desired effect when experienced from a distance.

The teacher must also recognize the limitation of words in the teaching of singing. A sound, even as a color, cannot be accurately described. Robert Louis Stevenson, a master of words, learned this fact when he wrote from Samoa to a London haberdasher hoping to duplicate the color of a favorite cravat. He decided that he could not make himself understood after several exchanges across a nineteenth century world slow in communication. There is a limitation of words in many aspects of teaching. The teacher must often seek another means of communication. If he does not, he will be adding to already existing confusions.

4

Feeling the Tone

The sensations associated with the production of vocal sound are difficult for the producer of the sound to describe. They are entirely personal, to some extent determined by previous experiences and sensations. The description of these sensations by successful singers are, therefore, varied. Regarding this, Joan Sutherland said, "You ask two singers how they get a particular note, and they will describe exactly opposite feelings — and what they are doing may be exactly the same thing."[1] However, there is a similarity in their descriptions when many are considered and summarized. In attempting to describe the feeling which they experience, vocalists may refer to vibratory sensations or they may refer to muscular sensations. Marilyn Horne stated it this way: "Singing is actually a series of sensations that one feels in one's body."[2] The descriptions by other singers may refer specifically to sensations associated with the head, the throat and mouth, the chest, or the lower thorax and abdomen. Here is a sampling of the kinds of things to which they refer:

---

[1]Richard Meryman, "A Tour of Two Great Throats," *Life*, Vol. 68, No. 24 (June 26, 1970) p. 68.

[2]*Ibid.*, p.66.

THE HEAD

"The tone feels high in the head and forward in the mask of the face."

"In the head register you resonate in the cavities of the head."

"The sound seems to come out here," the singer accompanying the statement with a hand gesture suddenly thrust forward from the forehead.

"I feel it here," the singer pointing to the forehead directly above the eyebrows.

"Everything is in the head."

"It all feels above my mouth."

"In the middle register you resonate in what we call the mask, nose, cheekbones, mouth and sinuses."[3]

THE THROAT AND MOUTH

A. VIBRATORY SENSATIONS.

"I feel nothing in my throat."

"When I sing, it feels as though I do not have a throat."

B. PHYSICAL SENSATIONS.

"Every singer must learn that relative position between the back of his tongue and his throat."

"The back of the roof of the mouth feels lifted."

---

[3]*Ibid.*, p.66. This description by Marilyn Horne closely resembles the description usually given by men.

"The sensation in the back of the mouth and throat resembles a suppressed yawn."

"The front of the throat seems to come forward."

"The tongue feels lowered and the roof of the mouth feels raised."

THE CHEST

Statements regarding the chest are less frequently encountered. The deepest tones of the female voice have often been designated as tones of the chest register, doubtless because of a frequently described feeling of chest vibration on low pitches. Singers acknowledge chest vibration on low tones but seldom speak of it, unprompted; probably because other sensations are more noticeable and more completely claim their attention. Here is one statement:

"When I sing in the chest register, if I were to put my hand on my chest, I could absolutely feel the vibrations terrifically."[4]

THE LOWER THORAX AND ABDOMEN

When sustaining a tone, successful singers experience and describe a feeling of firmness in the muscles which are used to expel the breath. This sensation has been usually termed "support" and a singer's description of the feeling seldom goes beyond the use of the word.

_____

The sensations brought about by correct singing have given rise to various methods of teaching. There are those which have attempted to arrive at the per-

_____

[4]*Ibid.*, p.66.

fect tone by striving for feelings in the mask of the face. Those based on this procedure have usually been referred to as methods of "tone placement." There are those which give attention to the physical sensations of the mouth and throat; they advocate such things as maintaining a forced smile, yawning as a means of opening the throat, and gaining a conscious control of the tongue. Just as the chest sensations have received little attention from singers, so have they from teachers, although the Italian singing master Sbriglia is reported to have always advocated keeping the tone in the chest.[5] Those methods which insist upon a consistently expanded and high position of the chest are in part based upon the recognition of chest resonance and in part upon an importance of breathing as related to singing. Of all the sensations which are described by singers, it seems that those which are related to the firmness of the breathing muscles while tone is being produced have been of the greatest interest to singing instructors. Their efforts to improve voices have been directed toward implanting the feeling of firmness in the lower part of the trunk of the body. Their method has been referred to as an approach through "proper breathing" and "diaphramatic support."

The shallowness and fallaciousness of thinking represented in many of these teaching practices is astonishing. If they were more successful in achieving their proposed results, we might, nevertheless, accept them as the means of arriving at beautiful singing. Since they are to a great extent unsuccessful, it may be well to examine them briefly; even a brief

---

[5]Orrin Luzern Huey, "Studying for the Great Tone," *Etude* (Philadelphia), Vol. 53, p.610.

consideration may reveal their unsound argument and make it apparent why they will continue to fail to consistently produce satisfactory results.

Let us first consider the basis of teaching which is founded upon "breath control." A brief explanation and an experiment may help to clarify thinking regarding this aspect of singing.

Every musical instrument consists of three functional parts: 1) a motor, 2) a vibrator, 3) a resonator. The motor mechanism of the voice is supplied by muscles of the lower ribs and the diaphragm pushing breath out of the lung cavity. The vocal cords which are the inner lips of the *thyro-arytenoid* muscles of the larynx are used as the vibrator. These lips, commonly referred to as cords, vibrate when they are drawn closely together by the muscles of the larynx and activated by the exhalation of breath. The resonator of the voice is provided by the cavities and certain hard surfaces in the upper part of the body.

We may draw a simplified comparison between the voice and a trumpet. The motor power of both is supplied by the exhalation of breath. The vibrator for the trumpet is furnished by the lips of the mouth, which, when pressed tightly together, serve the same function as that supplied by the lips of the *thryo-arytenoid* muscles (vocal cords) in the production of vocal sounds. Even the resonator of the voice has a certain similarity to the trumpet; cavities and hard surfaces of the upper part of the body add resonance to vocal sounds just as the tubular cavity and hard surface of the trumpet add resonance to trumpet sounds.

Keeping in mind the general similarity between the motor, vibrator, and resonator of both the voice and trumpet, let us now perform a simple experiment

45

in order that we may understand more thoroughly the relationship of "support" to vocal cord action. Press the lips tightly together and, while retaining the tight closure of the lips, expel breath. If the lips remain closed, the passing stream of breath will cause them to vibrate with a buzzing sound. Lip vibration, such as this, serves as the vibrator in trumpet playing. A similar buzzing of the lips of the larynx (vocal cords) serves as the vibrator in vocal production. When you create this buzzing sound by a firm closure of the lips you become conscious of a muscular action in the abdomen, lower back, and lower rib area; you become aware of the muscles which are forcefully expelling the breath. You may observe that this muscular action is much less noticeable when the breath is blown through *loosely* compressed lips. This muscular action in the abdominal area is one which is noticed by singers and trumpet players alike when they are producing sound correctly. These sensations, noted by good singers, have given origin to a belief that this is the keystone to singing.

Teachers who attack the vocal problem through breathing exercises and an artificial cultivation of "support" in the breathing apparatus are doing so with a belief that the "motor" feeling which good singers experience can be learned through a particular manner of inhalation and exhalation of the breath. They are considering this "support" of the tone to be a cause of correct vocal production. How incorrect their deduction is! The feeling which they observe is a *result* of the correctly produced tone, not a *cause.* The *cause* of the sensation to which they attach so much importance is the firm closure of the vocal cords which act in much the same manner as the consciously closed lips of the mouth acted when the experimenter pressed them tightly together in order to vibrate them.

From this experiment one other thing which has relationship to singing may be observed. When the lips are held tightly together and vibrated by the pressure of breath, the vibration may be sustained for a longer time than when the lips are but loosely compressed. So it is with singing. When the vocal cords are firmly approximated, the breath escapes very slowly through the tiny opening between the vibrating cords and the singer does not lack sufficient breath to sing melodic phrases of considerable length.[6] When the vocal cords fail to close with firmness, the breath is rapidly exhausted because it passes quickly between the cords which inadequately restrain it. The singer feels little or no "support" to the tone when the glottis, or opening between the cords, is not firmly closed. Conversely, "support" is felt when the muscles which close the glottis oppose the action of muscles which expel the breath from the lung cavity. In short, the action of the breath expelling muscles is firmly felt because they are meeting a resistance from the muscles closing the glottis. It is as though we are trying to keep the breath in by firmly pressing the vocal cords together and, at the

---

[6]When the cords are firmly together a very small quantity of breath, forcefully expelled, escapes between vibrations of the cords. A series of evenly spaced vibrations results in tone when sufficient breath pressure has forced the cords apart. The cords, from their own resiliency and the tension under which they are held, snap back to their original position only to be forced apart once more by the pressure of the breath. If the cords are not firmly and precisely closed, a larger quantity of less forcefully expelled breath escapes, resulting in loss of breath and inefficiency of tone production.

same time, trying to push the breath out. The sound has resulted from a slight overpowering of the muscles of the larynx by the very strong muscles of lower abdomen and diaphragm.

Teaching which is based upon an incorrect assumption will not only prove useless but in many instances will be harmful. If the action of the vocal cords is natural and correct, the feeling of "support" will be present and the singer will have enough breath to sustain long phrases. As for breathing, there will be little more to learn than when to breathe; how to breathe quickly and quietly; and how to breathe deeply. Many great singers have given no thought to breathing, and others have realized the danger in giving much consideration to this aspect of singing. The famous tenor Jussi Björling stated that the singer becomes short of breath when he begins to think of breathing.[7] Lauritz Melchior, renowned Wagnerian tenor, stated that breathing must be an entirely natural affair, that any constriction is wrong.[8] Frieda Hempel, one of the truly great operatic sopranos, wrote that the singer should not be bothered with complicated theories of breath support.[9]

Those who are thinking of "mask resonance" as the keystone to the beautiful voice are likewise engaged in oversight. Their thinking stems from the vibratory sensations which good singers notice in the upper face and head. The vibrations which the

---

[7]Jussi Björling, "Good Singing is Natural," *Etude* (Philadelphia) 1940, Vol. 58, p.655.

[8]Lauritz Melchior, "The 'Heldentenor' or Heroic Tenor," *Etude* (Philadelphia) 1937, Vol. 55, p.429.

[9]Frieda Hempel, "Sing with Your Heart!" *Etude* (Philadelphia) 1939, Vol. 57, p.229.

successful singer feels in the resonating area are present when the vocal cords function in proper manner and when the throat is not obstructed by an unnatural position of the tongue. If the voice is working correctly, the vibrations are usually felt in the face and head, but strong sensations are not felt there if the vocal cords are not pressed firmly together. This may be observed by the capable singer who normally feels the tone in the mask but finds that the resonance in that area is gone, or reduced, if he is suffering from a slight degree of laryngitis, and cannot, therefore, bring about a firm closure of the glottis. This will be noticed by the singer, even though the nasal passages may be clear. A remembrance of the head vibrations associated with good singing may be of great help to the singer who has experienced them; they may guide him in reproducing a correct tone. However, they cannot be considered the *cause* of the correct tone but only the *result* of a proper action of the vocal cords and a proper position of the throat. Many efforts to "place" the voice in the mask will fail because they will be based upon a false assumption that the tone can be directed into a particular area.

The description of tonal sensations by others has done little or nothing to help a student find the correct tone, unless that student has previously experienced the described sensations. If the student has not experienced the feelings, he does not understand a description of them and such descriptions do not, therefore, help him to sing better; they only cast an aura of mystery over the entire process of singing. The student does not understand the description because of a very obvious limitation of the human mind: **We are unable to understand any sensation** which we have not experienced ourselves. We are unable to truly understand *anything* which we have not in some way previously experienced. Failing to understand the sensation described by another, the student may entirely misinterpret the description. He is almost certain to lead himself into an even deeper state of confusion by trying to produce something which he does not understand.

Statements made by fine singers concerning the feelings which accompany their tonal production are not, by any means, useless. They furnish a valuable guide to the developing singer who in some way comes upon the correct tone. Having felt that tone, the singer comes, at least partially, to understand descriptions given by other singers. Their descriptions assist him in analyzing his own experience; they also give him assurance that he is proceeding correctly.

Thus it may be seen that that which is essential in learning to sing is not a wordy description of how to sing, or a detailed analysis of how a tone should sound and feel. The only thing of any importance, the only thing which will bring about the development of a beautiful voice is the personal experience associated with a properly produced tone. Something must be done to cause the singer to make a correct tone. Progress may be achieved if only one proper tone is formed. When the singer has produced such a tone and repeated and repeated it, and analyzed it, and come to know it, and been given assurance that this is the way he must use his voice, he is on his way toward the development of a beautiful and expressive voice. He then will come to know what his voice should **sound** like to himself, what his voice should **feel** like to himself!

5

Yes! There Are Registers

The existence of vocal registers was observed by some of the earliest vocal instructors. In fact, many teachers of the past gave more recognition to the existence of registers than those of the present. They often referred to three registers in the full compass of the voice; labeling them chest, middle, and head registers. However, even in the past there was controversy over the subject, some teachers declaring that there were as many as seven. The controversy continues; some teachers accepting registers as a natural physiologic action and others maintaining that registers do not exist. It seems to me a deluding blindness to disavow the existence of registers. It only appears to be an avoidance of what may be a troublesome problem in building the voice, the blending of registers. The refusal to accept and develop that which seems an obvious characteristic curtails the natural range, lessens the richness and strength of the voice, and leads to a variety of other faults. Faults invariably appear in the voice when it is used in an unnatural manner.

I think that it is manifest that two registers are present in the voices of men as well as those of women and that the full compass of the voice can only be realized when the registers are employed. The register phenomenon is not only to be observed in the human voice; it may be heard in the prolonged and inflected lowing of a cow, in the crowing of a rooster, in the baying of a hound! Those who refuse to recognize that there are registers usually maintain that the break in the voice is only the result of a maladjustment and not a natural physiologic action. Is it likely that all cows, roosters, and hounds suffer the same maladjustment? A smooth coordination between the registers is of no importance to the creatures which I have enumerated. It is, however, indispensable to the skilled singer. Fortunately it is a skill which is rather easily acquired if the singer at a reasonably early stage of life develops an independent usage of the two registers and then makes a conscious effort to develop a smoothness in joining them. As used here, the term "register" generally coincides with that given by Webster. Since misunderstandings often result from the terminology used in discussions of vocal problems, let me quote that definition: "A register is a series of tones of like quality within the compass of a voice which are produced by a particular adjustment of the vocal cords. In singing up the scale the register changes at the point where the singer readjusts the vocal cords to reach the higher notes. All below this point is in the chest register, all above it in the head register. The two registers generally overlap, some notes about the middle of the vocal range being producible in either." However, I choose to refer to the "head" register as *high* register and "chest" register as *low* register, feeling that some incorrect associations may be derived from the "chest" and "head" terminology.

The specific and complete muscular action involved in the production of each register is as yet not positively known. Observation by stroboscope and slow motion photography have shown a larger part of the vocal cords to be vibrating in the low register than in the high register. Although such observations are not made in natural circumstances, they furnish some indication that a tone may be produced by the thin edge of a small part of the vocal cords.[1] Electromyographic studies have also shown something of the relative activity of the *cricothyroid*, the *vocalis*, the *lateral* and the *interarytenoid* muscles in the separate registers and their blending.[2]

Although scientific studies may not have yet proven which muscles are principally involved in each of the registers, it does seem reasonable that the principal muscular emphasis is different for each of the registers and that the skill involved in making them work together requires a synergic action between the two muscles or two sets of muscles. Future experiments will unquestionably lead to further knowledge concerning the muscular actions involved in the production of the two registers and their coordination. Such knowledge may lead teachers to a more efficient means of developing and handling the registers of the voice. However, once again let it be said that it will only be of help if the teacher finds a means of applying the scientific knowledge to the practical needs of the singer. Such knowledge in itself will be of no more value to the singer than knowledge concerning the activity of the *latissimus dorsi* muscle is to the golfer.

---

[1] The slow motion pictures taken by the Bell Laboratories show this to be the case in a small "falsetto" tone produced by the male voice.

[2] William Vennard, Minoru Hirano, and John Ohala, "Laryngeal Synergy in Singing," *The NATS Bulletin*, Vol.XXVII, No. 1 October 1970, p.16.

The important thing for the singer is a thorough acquaintance with the two registers of the voice and correct usage of both. The natural voice will never be achieved until the singer has found it in both of these registers. If it is found in one register only, the voice may be handled well within a comparatively short range but at least one half of the complete voice will be faulty or entirely lacking. The singer will be directing his voice toward its greatest possible development if he learns to separate the two registers; finds the correct manner of producing both; seeks to employ these separated registers in the extremities of his range; and then makes them work together in that area where they overlap.

If we consider the entire field of songs and arias written for the human voice, we cannot fail to observe that the complete expression of these songs places tremendous vocal requirements upon the singers who undertake them. There are vocalists who, through interest in a particular style, or because of vocal or artistic limitations, have specialized in the performance of only one type of song. There are others who have proven the magnificent versatility of the human voice and their own emotional sensitivity by performing almost every style of vocal solo. Singing of this type demands a range of at least two octaves for men and more for women. In addition to this, it requires great strength, delicacy, flexibility, virtuosity, endurance, control of dynamics and sustained tone, and a quality which is agreeable and expressive. Such singing is possible and should be the goal of every singer.

Unlike the instrumentalist, the singer cannot separate himself from the instrument upon which he plays. It is his very own. He should be ambitious to develop it to the fullest extent in order that he may fully express himself. The separate employment and coordinated use of both registers is essential to that full development of the voice. They are used by the greatest of singers, but many aspiring singers fail to realize this. They fail to adequately develop the registers, thereby limiting their performance. It seems incredible that this development should be neglected. What serious pianist would buy a piano with half of a keyboard, or limit his efforts to playing with only one hand when two extend his possibilities?

Once again let us look to human mentality and the social customs with which we have surrounded ourselves. These customs, a product of mentality, have much to do with the usual development of one register of the voice: the upper in men's voices and the lower in the voices of women.

The high register in the male voice reaches far into the range of women's voices and consequently has a quality which is associated with the female voice. Since men are respected for their masculinity, the average man avoids the cultivation of effeminate mannerisms. He avoids an employment of the upper half of his voice because it is thought to be effeminate. The consequent lack of use over an extended time brings about a debilitation of the muscles involved in producing that register. The resulting weakness hampers the natural working of the voice. If the average male reaches adulthood with a developed upper register it is quite by accident. If he has continued singing while his voice was changing, he may have retained some of the high register, since that was the register he was probably most often using when the voice commenced to deepen. Sometimes he has retained or even developed this part of the voice because he has been associated with a certain occupation, or ethnic group, where employment of the high register has been traditional; for example, people of the open spaces, such as American cowboys or Swiss mountaineers, use this voice in calls or in yodeling. Russian and English choristers, singing the higher parts, have also used the upper register to extend the compass of their all male choirs. Thus the forces of social custom may again be seen; men have no hesitation in using this voice if it is used by others of their group.

Women have usually neglected the low register, rather than the high, and for a similar reason. The low register in a woman's voice suggests the quality of the male voice. Women avoid being thought masculine by avoiding this part of the voice. Yet both registers are natural to both sexes. They are a part of the voice which has been given to us and, if we are to use the voice correctly, we must employ its registers.

The male and female voices are remarkably similar in nature. Why should they not be? The mechanism is the same and the male larynx and resonance chambers are only slightly larger. However, the slightly larger size of larynx, vocal cords, and resonance chambers causes the complete range of the male voice to be approximately one octave lower than the female voice. Both the male and female voices have an upper and lower register which overlap on approximately the same notes of the scale. When both voices are thoroughly developed, the heavier voices of women and the lighter voices of men sound very much alike when sounding the same pitch.

Social forces and the predominance of low register combine to make that register the principal one used by men in speaking and singing.

Social custom and the predominance of the high register in female voices have resulted in the more frequent employment of that register by women. However, there are exceptions such as the female singer of popular songs who, because of a current fashion, often sings almost exclusively in her low register. Such a fad may be responsible for young girls developing the low register and neglecting the upper. Imbalance of registers is also the case with many stage actresses who have learned to make themselves heard in large theatres by speaking in the low voice. Persistent use of the low register by actresses and young girls often results in extraordinary development of that register, indicating the extent to which it can be developed. However, many who develop this part of the voice neglect the upper, and because of that neglect eventually encounter serious vocal problems.

The accompanying chart (Figure 1) illustrates the approximate compass of the registers and the range of the male and female voices when both registers are developed. The extremities indicated in the chart can be advanced to a further degree by constant practice. Taxing the absolute extremities of the upper register, however, is probably unwise since there could be little or no use made of such range.

The role played by the individual registers in the complete range of the voice should be observed in the chart. It will be seen that the low register in the tenor voice, for example, can be developed to the extent of two octaves or more. It is capable of sounding notes well below C^2 [footnote 3] and may also be used to reach tones in the neighborhood of B flat above C^3. If it is used by itself to produce tones above G^3, a noticeable strain will be placed on the voice; the strain will be apparent in sound and feeling. The diagram shows

57

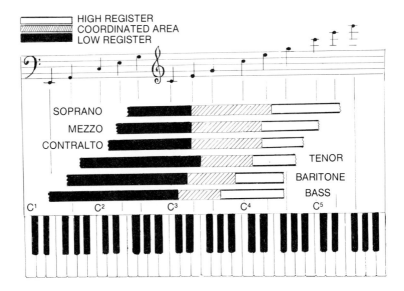

Figure 1. — Illustrating the approximate range of fully developed, correctly produced voices. The chart also illustrates the approximate range of the individual registers and the coordinated area between the registers.

also that the high register has a range of approximately one and one-half octaves which extend from the neighborhood of C³ to the vicinity of F⁴ sharped. If properly developed, this register will be very strong in the upper half of its range. By persistent practice one may gain a fair amount of strength in its lower half, but a weakness and breathiness in the lowest notes will make an exclusive use of this part of the register

---

[3]The numeral used here for pitch identification indicates the position of the note on the piano keyboard. The lowest C on the keyboard is simply labeled C. The next above that is C¹, the second above that lowest C is C² etc. See Figure 1 which also indicates the pitch by means of staff notation.

seem strange and unnatural. However, these lowest notes of the high register should be developed because of the part which they play in blending the two registers. You will observe from the diagram that there is an overlapping of the registers, approximately one octave may be produced by either register. However, the registers are not normally used independently within this octave. The skilled singer coordinates them so that the voice passes smoothly from the low to the high. If he has developed and used both registers, he can sing from his lowest tones to his highest, covering a span of approximately three octaves, without an abrupt or noticeable change in quality.

The same action of the registers is natural to the baritone and bass voices. Somewhat surprisingly the range of these voices and the bridge between the registers is only slightly lower than that of the tenor voice.

It is interesting to observe that the overlapping of registers in both the female and male voices takes place on approximately the same notes of the scale. This transition, however, lies in a different area of women's voices than of men's. Since the complete range of the female voice is approximately one octave higher than that of the male voice, the transition between registers lies in the lower part of the female singing range and in the upper part of that range which men employ in public singing. This creates a very much more difficult problem in men's voices than in women's.

When a fine coordination between registers exists, it has usually been gained over a long period of time, beginning early in the person's life. Such coordination is highly desirable in women's voices and should be an objective. Lack of a smooth coordination, however, has not deterred many women from successful careers. Many famous female vocalists have never overcome a noticeable change in quality between the two registers and yet they have achieved fame and artistic success as singers. Such change in quality in the lower part of women's voices, although it should not be approved, has generally been accepted.

Faulty coordination between the registers of a woman's voice may be overlooked because melodic climaxes seldom occur in the low part of the voice. However, the great vocal climaxes written for men involve those tones that lie within the area of register coordination. The coordination must be good. If it is not, the tones are strained, weak, or of different quality and the listener finds only disappointment in the climax.

From this it may be seen that coordination between the registers is an important part of the great singer's skill, perhaps even more important for men than for women. When the exercises of this book are presented it will become apparent that a full development of both registers is of equal importance to men and women alike and an essential factor in the maximum development of their voices.

6

The Labyrinth and the Golden Thread

The problems confronting the vocal instructor are unusual and challenging. He is faced with the task of rectifying confusions and misconceptions. He is opposed by psychological barriers which he must try, at least in part, to dissolve or bypass. He must in some way bring the singer to a feeling of the correct tone and a remembrance of the sound of that tone, but, in this most important and subtle phase of his teaching, he can find little help from words.

An ancient myth tells of the minotaur, a vicious beast kept in a bewildering labyrinth in the great palace at Knossos. When the handsome Theseus came to Crete for the purpose of slaying the minotaur he was assisted by Ariadne. She gave him a golden thread and warned him of the immense difficulty in finding a way out of the intricate labyrinth. Accepting the assistance of Ariadne he marked his pathway into the labyrinth by laying down the thread. After having killed the threatening monster, he had but to follow the thread to find his way back to the world he had left behind.

Most vocal students are lost in a labyrinth constructed from their own confusion. Lacking direction for their learning they go one way and another, even in circles, and are totally unable to find the path that will lead them back to a voice which since childhood has been lost to them. They have an abundance of ideas and impressions concerning vocal sounds but their concepts are usually false and misleading. The teacher who is to help cannot possibly know all that is contributing to the vocal problem. The influences which may have shaped the thinking of the aspiring singer and formed his concepts regarding vocal tone are infinite. They exert an invisible force upon the working of the voice. They are obscure to the teacher, and, to a great extent, to the singer himself. They are one of the greatest obstacles to the teacher's efforts to implant a correct image of tone production. Some of the imprint in the mind of the student may be revealed to the teacher in the course of time, but much of it lies buried so deeply in the student's subconscious that even he has no awareness of it or its effect upon his voice. He has little remembrance of the origin of the thoughts which he has concerning tone production. Some of his ideas may have come from the words of a vocal instructor, some may have come from a book concerning singing, but it is quite certain that many of his impressions and beliefs were implanted long before he visited a vocal teacher or took down a book from the library shelf.

The vocal student's fears place an additional difficulty in the path of his teacher. In the delicately coordinated muscular activity of singing, *fear* can be a dragon with a hundred heads reared against the success of the undertaking. It can scatter the forces of concentration, bind the suppleness and power of muscles, and destroy the concerted effort. Every singer at some time and to some degree must overcome this enemy. The singer's most direct means of combating this threat to his success is the elimination of weaknesses from his performance. Probably the most worrisome part of his singing is the action of the voice itself. If he can succeed in establishing a firm technique, a sureness in the production of the tone, he will have done much in gaining a confidence that can help him in casting aside his fears. These fears, however, are not only present before an audience; they are with him at the outset of his studio training and stand between him and his desire to use the voice correctly. In helping to alleviate these fears, the teacher must have sympathetic understanding of the singer's sensitivity and assist him in every way to gain the confidence necessary to him as a singer.

To some extent almost everyone is timid. All about us we see the effect which timidity has upon the individual. Some are dreadfully shy; they avoid other people, they turn their eyes downward, and they speak in a whisper. The extremely shy person finds it difficult to learn to sing effectively. However, he will find that any success achieved with his voice will be helpful to him in overcoming his diffidence. Voice and personality are closely intermingled. Many find that a release of their voices liberates other aspects of their personalities. Overcoming vocal inhibitions brings confidence and courage which is helpful in other aspects of one's life. The natural shyness of the average person may have affected the voice but it will by no means prevent the learning of correct vocal usage.

That which appears to be an extroverted personality is sometimes only a disguise for inherent shyness. Such a person, as well as the true extrovert, talks in a loud authoritative voice. In his desire to be loud he may have misused his voice and created problems, but he will probably have less trouble in learning to sing than the person who is extremely timid. The extrovert, even if his extroversion is only a masquerade, will not be afraid to project his voice.

The personal nature of the sensations associated with correct vocal usage gives added difficulty to the teacher. As previously explained, words are of little use in giving the student any real understanding of these sensations. We cannot divine how another will describe the experience. Can we truly describe our own sensations? Only in the vaguest manner are we able to find words to define them.

How then can the teacher, facing all of these difficulties, proceed to help the student if words give little assistance?

My firm belief that the great singer is doing nothing more than producing a tone in the natural manner leads me to believe that we are only seeking to use the voice as nature intended. If the student can be brought to emit a completely natural sound, he should be able to analyze it and learn to apply that kind of tone to his singing. If he does, he will have made a detour around the misconceptions which are blocking his progress and will be able to proceed directly toward his goal. I see no other way of conveying the feeling and the proper sound to the student than through the free emission of natural sounds. Those sounds which I have found to be useful cannot be described and could not, therefore, be transmitted in a book if it were not possible to include a recording of them. Those which have been selected are aimed at finding that completely free vocal production which seems instinctive with animals and human beings alike. The student will arrive at this natural sound more quickly if he disassociates it from his accustomed voice. By so doing, he will, to some extent, be able to bypass the hampering misunderstandings which have previously blocked his effort to use his voice properly. When first heard, the sounds may seem entirely unrelated to correct singing or speaking, but a closer analysis will disclose characteristics which are also present in the voices of great singers and speakers. The tones are clear, they are freely produced, they are strong and far carrying, they lack breathiness, they are rich with fundamental and overtones. When they are accurately imitated, the producer of the tone experiences sensations which have been described by great singers and speakers of the past and present. The student comes, through these sounds, to know the feeling of the natural tone, and he then has but to listen to himself to know the sound which he must associate with a properly used voice. It is a simple, direct, positive approach to a problem that may otherwise be extremely complicated.

The sounds which are reproduced on the recording are directly related to the kind of sound used by great singers. If the aspiring singer cannot learn to imitate these sounds, he or she cannot use the voice well. The great singer may never have knowingly made such sounds as these but he or she would have no difficulty in doing so. I am sure that they are not the only sounds that could be directed to this purpose but their effectiveness has been proven to me. I offer them with confidence in their helpfulness. They are able to serve the singer as the golden thread served Theseus. Through them the singer is enabled to find his way out of the labyrinth.

7

Exercises for the Development of the Voice

How To Use The Recorded Sounds

FOR THE FEMALE VOICE
AND THE UNCHANGED BOY'S VOICE

Exercise 1. *Hoo-ee.*

Hoo-ee   Hoo-ee   Hoo-ee   Hoo-ee

Raise the volume control on your amplifier until the sound approximates that of a very loud voice. Listen carefully to the recording. Press your ear close to the source of sound in order that you may better understand how this exercise would sound if you were very close to the person producing it. This will give you a better understanding of how it may sound to yourself.

Now try to produce the sound. You may at first be self conscious and embarrassed to call out in such fashion. You will do better if you are alone or in the presence of one who understands. If you make the sound correctly, the tone will have great carrying power but you must not have fear of creating disturbance. You cannot successfully achieve the desired results if you try to hold the tone within, if you are afraid that you will be heard. Do not think of this as singing. Imagine that you are calling to someone at a great distance, that you are not at first heard and you call again and again, each time trying harder to be heard. Do not strain to produce the sound. Hear the sound in your mind — listen again to the recording and then let your voice go. Rejoice in the feeling that you are releasing a great power which is yours, that you are breaking the chains that have imprisoned your voice.

If you feel that you have been successful in imitating the sound, try to analyze it. Do you feel the tone in your head? Does it seem to come out of your forehead? Do you feel pressure at the diaphragm? Whatever your sensations are, remember them!

Execute this call at various pitches and find that pitch where you seem to be able to do it most successfully. It is important that you learn to release this high part of your voice but it is not important that it, at first, comes out freely on each of the pitches demonstrated on the recording. Do not perform the exercises on pitches higher or lower than those which are demonstrated.

If you have been successful, you will have had some indications that you were right. The sound will have been made without strain, without discomfort in the throat. It will have been emitted with great strength but it will not have seemed to you that this power resulted from forcing. It will have seemed that the tone released quickly, that there was neither slowness nor sluggishness in the attack. You will certainly have felt some satisfaction in sensing a liberation of your voice, but the sound of the tone will have probably bewildered you.

At this point you need either the assistance of a person who is experienced in hearing correct vocal tones, or a well made recording of the sounds which you have made. You must know whether or not you have been successful in imitating the recorded sounds. Some may be able to imitate the sound after a few attempts, others may take longer.

If you have not been successful, you must continue to try, remembering to do it vigorously but without an uncomfortable strain. If your voice has been badly misused, you will probably be handicapped by a weakness of vocal muscles, as well as established patterns of incorrect muscular action. It may take you weeks to learn to effectively produce this one sound. Do not be discouraged. If you persevere, you can learn to do this and you will be rewarded for your efforts. Proceed to Exercises 2 and 3, they may help you to find this initial and very important sound.

Even after you have been successful in imitating the sound you must repeat it again and again, pausing between each effort; first, to recall the feeling and the sound which you have experienced, and second, to prepare for the next attack by a remembrance of those feelings and that sound. It is necessary that you remember the sensations which you associate with this tone; they will become the guiding light in your future use of the voice.

It is likely, that your first attempts will be only partially successful. You will probably be inconsistent in your trials; it is almost certain that some tones will come out better than others. You must learn to be consistent. It cannot be assumed that you have mastered this sound until every attempt is successful. It is probable that the sounds will be comparable to those of the recording but will not equal them in clarity, freedom, power, or precision of attack. Persist with your practicing. Play the recording, imitating each *Hoo-ee* during the time lapse between sounds. Listen carefully and try to be exact in your imitation.

Do not be alarmed, if at first an occasional effort to call the tone induces coughing and a scratching or pulling sensation in the throat. Such discomfort would certainly indicate that you have done something incorrectly. I would suspect that the extrinsic muscles of the larynx, which hold the voice box in its proper position, have not functioned properly, thereby causing the feeling of strain. The action of these muscles will be discussed in later chapters. If such strain is felt, remember that anyone learning a skill is going to be unsuccessful with some attempts. The strain must be eliminated as quickly as possible but a few unsuccessful efforts are not going to damage your voice. The vocal mechanism is not that fragile. Simply pause for a few moments in your practicing, and learn to execute Exercise 2. If the *Hoo-ee* is then preceded by the inhaling sound demonstrated for that exercise, the uncomfortable feeling will probably vanish. The discomfort of which I speak is felt by very few who try to make this sound and is experienced only by them in a few of the first attempts.

Review these instructions several times. Strive for perfection in the sounds which you make. It is not an exercise which you are to practice for a week; it is a guide to your basic technique and an exercise which may serve you for years to come. If you are successful in doing it, you will have found a teacher in this sound. It will be able to tell you something concerning the use of your voice that no person can put into words. The notation of the exercise is given. However, at first it is better that you imitate the recorded sound without regard to pitch. If the notes are played on the piano, you are more apt to think of the exercise as singing. If the notes are approached as singing, you will probably perform them as usual. We are hoping to by-pass misconceptions and build the singing voice upon the foundations of the natural voice. Strive for that voice and try to forget your customary manner of making tone.

Exercise 2. *Inhaling Sound.*

This sound is produced by vibrating the vocal cords while the breath is being inhaled. It has nothing directly to do with singing but is usually of value in learning to sing. When it is properly made, the *hyoglossus* muscle has contracted. The contraction of this muscle is of great importance in the production of resonant vocal sound; its contraction causes a downward tilting of the front of the *hyoid* bone and an opening of the throat through tongue action. If this exercise proves helpful to you it is because it has brought about a proper placement of the *hyoid* bone and has set the tongue in its correct position for tone production. If this has happened, it will have given a feeling of openness at that place where the back of the mouth joins the throat. This physical sensation is one that the expert vocalist usually associates with correct tone production.

Care should be taken, in doing this exercise, not to lower the larynx. If the larynx is being lowered, you can detect the lowering movement by pressing the forefinger against the top segment of the *trachea* (windpipe) just below the larynx (see Figure 27). A lowering of the larynx will cause a deeper, more hollow sound than that produced with the larynx in normal position. The voice cannot function properly with the larynx greatly displaced, and, because of the risk of improper habit formation, no exercise should be regularly performed with the larynx in an unnatural position.

Use this exercise in association with Exercise 1. After making the inhaling sound one or more times, you should call the *Hoo-ee*. If, after doing this exercise, the called *Hoo-ee* comes out more clearly and with greater ease, the exercise may be considered useful. If it seems to have no beneficial effect upon the called tone, there is no reason for continuing it as a regular exercise. However, it should be tried from time to time in the hope that it may become helpful.

An exercise such as this approaches the problem of tone production in an unnatural and reverse manner. A physical feeling is considered before the desired sound is summoned from the mind. The natural process first brings to mind the impression of sound which is to be physically created and it is this which gives impulse to the muscular action. However, some people who are handicapped in using their voices have, through improper vocal thinking, or poor speech, established an interfering habit of tongue action. The habit is so ingrained with these individuals that it becomes impossible for them to produce the desired clear call. Little can ordinarily be accomplished by consciously trying to control the tongue. However, if through this exercise you are able to bring about the desired throat sensation, it is likely that the tongue will remain in a favorable position long enough to allow production of an improved sound. If you are successful in producing the correct tone, progress will be made in establishing the desired mental impression. After the mental impression is established, the correct muscular action will stem from that source, which is the natural and correct one.

Exercise 3. *Sharp attack on Hoo.*

Little explanation of this exercise seems necessary. Listen to the sound and imitate it. Do it with spontaneity! It may have a similarity to certain animal or bird sounds. Why should it not? Why should there not be a similarity between some human and some animal sounds, if the sound is a natural one?

If you are successful in making the sound, return to Exercise 1 and try to apply the same kind of attack. Strive for the same freedom.

Exercise 4 *The Hum.*

Humming is frequently used as an exercise for the cultivation of the voice. Often it is used without considering whether or not it is correctly produced. Humming is customarily described as singing with the lips closed. The definition, like the definition of singing, is an extreme simplification; it does not distinguish good from poor vocal utterance. The mere closing of the lips gives no assurance that the hum will be a correct one. Incorrect tones can be made with the mouth closed, just as they may be made with the mouth open.

I believe that there is but one way to produce the completely natural human sound. All of the recorded exercises are intended as examples of this sound. I also believe that the throat is open to the utmost when sound is free, and that the maximum throat opening is achieved by pressing forward the posterior portion of the tongue. Unfortunately, this action cannot be seen. The action is illustrated in Figure 23 and discussed further in Chapter Eleven. Furthermore, I believe that (1) that portion of the tongue remains in essentially the same position for all well executed sounds; (2) correctly produced vowels are but variations of the basic natural sound; (3) they are formed without change of this posterior tongue position. It is possible to alter the position of the lips, jaw, and that part of the tongue which lies in the mouth without altering the position of the rear portion of the tongue. The correctly produced natural sound may be made with the mouth in different positions but the rear portion of the tongue must be in the position previously described. If a singer produces a correctly formed middle or lower range sound with the mouth in its most open position, the sound will take the form of an AH. This vowel will change to OO, if the tongue placement is unchanged and the mouth is altered to a rounded and only slightly opened position. If the tongue still remains unchanged in position and the mouth is then completely closed, the sound will become a resonant and correctly produced hum.

The rather unusual sound on the recording is the natural sound produced with the mouth closed; the same basic sound used for any correctly formed vowel.

Since the hum of the recording has proven its value, and since a variety of hums can be made, it is important that you know whether or not you are successfully imitating the recorded sound. Again you must depend upon a recording of your voice or the reliable ear of another to tell you. However, you may have certain indications of correctness. Almost invariably the successful producer of this sound will notice vibrations in the general area of the nose. This sensation is an indication of correctness but not an infallible guide with vocal sounds, since some incorrect tones may be felt in the nose. With the hum, however, strong vibration in the nose or mask may be taken as indication that the hum has been correctly made. With the mouth closed the tone will be badly blocked and muffled unless the back of the tongue is down and forward. If correctly produced, it will not seem to be pushed up from the throat but rather to originate higher than the mouth, with the vibrations felt in the upper face rather than on the lips. The sound will be stronger and more free than the usual hum and will probably be very strange to your ears. These are general descriptions of the sensations experienced by others. Do not strive for these sensations. Try to imitate the sound and compare your results with these descriptions.

If you are not successful in producing the sound, pass on to the next exercise but return frequently to this. You may discover it through persistence.

Exercise 5. *Repeated Hum and Repeated Hoo.*

This sound is the same as that of Exercises 3 and 4 but it is executed with a sharp staccato. Perform the exercise lightly. Strive for a tone which seems to originate high in the head. Be sure that the attack is swift and clean. Do not slide into the tone but strive for a precise attack, one which immediately finds the pitch heard in your mind. The sound may suggest to you the whimpering of a puppy or the sound of a baby; these too are natural sounds.

Exercise 6. *The short Hoo-ee.*

This exercise, which is essentially the same sound as that of Exercise 1, is referred to as the *Short Hoo-ee* because of the quick release of the first tone. It is performed as an octave skip rather than as the major third of Exercise 1 but it should be approached as a call to be imitated, not as an interval to be sung. Notice the sharp precision of the attack; it is important. This explosive attack is the result of a firm closure of the glottis. The vocal cords are pressed tightly together before breath is expelled. Through these exercises you are indirectly learning to bring about a firm closure of the glottis. This proximity of the vocal cords will give brilliance and strength to the voice.

The closed vowels OO and EE are used for these exercises because, with them, it seems easier to achieve the desired basic sound. These vowels are referred to as closed vowels because the mouth is more closed in making them than it is in making OH or AH. By using closed vowels for the development of the upper voice you are more apt to experience the sensation of head vibrations. Awareness of such vibrations will be very helpful to you in acquiring the greatest freedom and beauty in the upper register. Because of the semi-closed position of the mouth it will only be possible to produce these vowels with freedom if the back of the tongue is in a low position. The cultivation of that tongue position, without conscious effort, will result in the most desirable quality and ease of production for all vowels.

In the early stages of development you will very likely find that the sound comes out best on a particular note in the range. It is important that you find the note where you can execute the sound most successfully. An attempt is being made through these sounds to implant an image of correct vocal sound. The pitch is not of any great importance since any successful effort will be enlightening to you. However, to ensure acquaintance with the high register, the pitch should be above E on the top space of the treble clef. After practicing this sound for a few weeks, or perhaps less time, it may be discovered that the sound comes out best on a slightly higher pitch. This gradual rise in the pitch may continue until the attack is on a high B or C. If it is performed correctly, you will notice that you are able to repeat dozens of these calls without an apparent tiring of the voice. The highest pitches should never be intentionally sought; the voice should be allowed to come out on the pitch where you find the greatest release.

If the voice does not release freely and easily in performing this exercise, you should not regularly do it but should persist with Exercise 1. However, you should occasionally return to this *Short Hoo-ee,* only accepting it as a regular part of your practice routine when it is performed with ease. If that ease can be found, the exercise will be of great value in establishing the highest part of the range.

Exercise 7. *Ay Ay Ay* (pronounced as *i* in ice)

Ay Ay Ay Ay Ay Ay Ay Ay   Ay   Ay Ay Ay Ay Ay Ay Ay Ay   Ay

Up to this point all exercises intended for women have been in the upper register. I believe that we should begin with the higher register, learning to completely separate it from any coordination with the low. This separation is an action which in singing becomes necessary for the acquisition of freedom in the upper range of the voice.

The lower limits of a register are not abruptly reached. Weakness and breathiness of tone continue to increase as a singer approaches the lowest note of the register. When women sing in the high register exclusively, their middle range is usually deficient, the lower tones are breathy and lacking in resonance, and the lowest tones written for their voice classification are entirely lacking. Often, in an effort to give greater body to their low tones, they create an artificial darkening of the voice. They deceive themselves; the tone sounds fuller to them but its lack of clarity eliminates carrying power. Tones produced in this way are not only ineffective in themselves but also upsetting to the correct production of higher tones. In the production of effective tones capable of expressive quality throughout a wide range, it is essential that the singer develop both registers of the voice.

In order to become acquainted with the low register and to develop it, the singer should search below the limits of the high register. It is for this reason that the exercise given for low register development (Exercise 7) begins on A below the middle C of the piano keyboard.

The use of open vowel sounds (OH, AH, Ā) seem better suited than the closed vowels (EE and OO) for the first efforts to develop the low register. The diphthong AY is recommended for this exercise because it is more likely to lead to the desired projection of sound. There is a prevalent tendency to retract the tongue in an effort to darken low tones. This is unnecessary, harmful, and hampering to the full development of any part of the voice. The extreme brightness of the recorded sounds should be observed. To produce the sound you should open the mouth from one to one and one-half inches and, without moving the jaw, sing loudly with a quality which seems metallic and extremely clear to your own ears. In producing the sound you should avoid an up and down movement of the jaw. The widely opened but immobile jaw will compel tongue movement for the formation of the diphthong, activating the *hyoglossus* muscle and contributing to a flexibility in the use of the tongue.

Once again your efforts must be appraised; either by someone who can tell you whether or not you are duplicating the recorded sound, or by yourself with the assistance of a recorder. If you are doing the exercise correctly the tone will seem firm and strong, the production will be free and easy, and, even if you have a very high voice, you will be able to transpose the exercise by half steps and comfortably reach the E below the piano's middle C.

It may be advisable to postpone work in developing the low part of the voice if the low register is already stronger than the high register or if you find that the upper tones come out less well after practicing in the low register. If that is the case, continue practicing the exercises for the high register until that part of the technique is securely founded. After the upper voice seems to be secure, resume practicing in the low register, but for brief periods only.

EXERCISES FOR THE MALE VOICE

Exercise 1M.   *No! Potatoes! Tomatoes! Hello!*
Many years have now passed since my student days in New York, but I recall clearly the sounds of a vegetable hawker as he made his daily round with horse drawn wagon. Each day there came the cry, "tomatoes! potatoes!" from a block away and over a multitude of city sounds, through the cavernous streets of a Manhattan apartment house district. Even at that time before I had considered teaching singing, I knew that there was something right about the manner in which this man used his voice and I knew that it had a resemblance to the great sounds which I heard at the Metropolitan Opera. His voice was easily heard, and because it was heard he sold his vegetables. Little strain was placed upon his voice, despite the hours of use, and this enabled him to sell on another day. When I checked the pitch of his call I usually found it to be on a high F sharp. It was not dissimilar to the sounds which are recorded as Exercise 1M.

Carefully read the general instructions for Exercise 1 for women's voices. Those instructions are also applicable for Exercise 1M and should be understood by all men who undertake this exercise.

Listen carefully to the sound and then proceed to imitate it. Do not sing the tone. Call out as though you are striving to make yourself heard at a great distance. If the example seems too high or too low for your voice, produce it on another pitch, one which seems best for you. It is not important that the sound be made on the same pitch as the recorded example; it is only important that you discover the correct sound. Do not be disturbed by the tonal quality; remember that you cannot properly judge that. Find the easiest manner of producing it. If you are successful, you will probably have a feeling that there is great strength and authority in your voice. You will have exerted yourself in making the sound but it will have seemed to have been emitted with ease.

If you produce this sound correctly, it will undoubtedly do much in establishing your basic vocal technique. Even after that technique is established, the exercise should always be used to remind you of the sensations associated with a correctly produced tone. The great American baritone John Charles Thomas, late in his career, was still calling a similar sound for just that purpose. It is, of course, of the utmost importance that you do this correctly and you may need the help of another to determine whether your imitation is close to that of the recorded sound.

Exercise 2M.   *The Inhaling Sound.*

Read the explanation given for Exercise 2 for female voices; it is also applicable for this exercise.

Use this exercise in association with Exercise 1M. Call the "No," as demonstrated for that exercise, immediately after making the inhaling sound. This exercise is used for the purpose of inducing the correct position of the tongue. If it is made immediately before calling the "No" it may bring the tongue into a proper position, thereby improving the tone that is to follow. If it is of assistance, the "No" will immediately come out to some degree more clearly and comfortably. If there is indication that the exercise is helpful it should be continued.

Exercise 3M.   *Hoo-ee.*

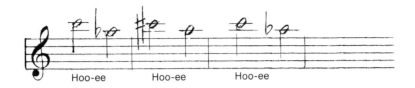

The upper register in men's voices has almost invariably been neglected to a greater extent than the low. If you have made no use of the upper register for years, you may expect that it will take some time to become acquainted with it, to strengthen it, and to bring it back into the natural functioning of your voice. For the full development and proper functioning of the male voice it is absolutely essential that the high register be developed.

The first step in gaining acquaintance with the high register may be made by imitating the recording of Exercise 3M. Release this sound with spontaneity. Once again, project it as though you were desirous of being heard at a distance and do it on that pitch of your voice where it seems to come out most easily. After you have acquired the ability to produce such a sound, you may proceed to develop the high register. Persistent practice over a period of months will give you great power and an astonishing range in this register of the voice.

You must strive for full-bodied clarity and for complete comfort in the throat. A pinched sound and a constrained pulling sensation in the throat must be avoided. It should not feel as though the tone had been directed into the mouth. If you are producing the sound correctly, it is almost certain that you will describe this tone as being felt somewhere above the mouth; in the upper part of the face, or perhaps it may seem to go straight up into the head.

Your first successful tones in this register will probably be found in the neighborhood of the male high C (C⁴), although they may be as low as A³ or as high as F⁴. The pitch at which the tone is found is not of importance; it only matters that the correct sound be discovered. After it has been found and strengthened in the upper half of the register, it is advisable that systematic practice be applied toward the development of the lower notes of the register. To do this you should carry the high register down into its lowest possible notes, taking care that the low register is not employed. Always try to eliminate breathiness and strive for as much resonance as possible. Avoidance of any blending of the registers in this exercise will hasten the development of the high register.

In some instances the singer may have become so confused in his use of the upper register, or may have neglected it to such an extent, that he will find great difficulty in learning to use it. If the low register seems to function less well after practicing in the upper voice, it is almost certainly an indication of incorrect practice in the high register. Should this situation be encountered, it would be better to either postpone your efforts to develop the high voice or to practice it for very short periods of time, alternately returning to the low register exercises.

A Practice Routine for Men

You are advised to immediately read Chapter Nine concerning the blending of registers. You should add the exercises for development of coordination between the registers as soon as you have learned to produce high register tones. It is recommended that a routine of practice should be established as soon as you are able to execute the descending two octave scale (Exercise 4M) and the ascending nine-tone scale (Exercise 5M). Assuming that you are able to do Exercise 3M without difficulty, I would recommend that a few minutes of each practice period (there could be many in one day) be devoted to each of the following exercises and that they be done in this order:

1. Exercise 3M *(Hoo-ee)*
2. Exercise 4M *(Descending two octave scale)*
3. Exercise 5M *(Ascending nine-tone scale)*
4. Exercise 1M *(Called No!)*
5. Exercise 6M *(No, sung on descending arpeggio)*

I advise placing the upper register exercises and those intended to bring about coordination between the registers at the beginning of the practice session because of the importance of register coordination. If a man is able to separate the registers and also able to sing smoothly from one to the other, he will never know many of the vocal problems commonly associated with the male voice.

If, through these exercises, you have been successful in finding an easy manner of producing both registers, you are well on the way toward the acquisition of a beautiful and expressive voice which will be extensive in range. Applying the sounds which you have made to singing is our next concern.

EXERCISES FOR THE DEVELOPMENT
OF THE SPEAKING VOICE

I think that it is now apparent that there is really only one correct way to use the voice. It is determined by the complete scheme of things, by the balances within our body, by the intention of that mysterious thing which I have repeatedly referred to as Nature! There is not one right way to use the speaking voice and another right way to use the singing voice. The basically correct manner of using the voice must be found — it serves for our daily communication just as it serves for the accomplished singer.

What divides speech from song? Sometimes it is narrowly divided, sometimes it is overlapped, sometimes it is not divided at all. I suppose the simplest definition would be that song is sustained and speech is not, that the singer prolongs vowels on a specific pitch, and the speaker does not. Like most simple definitions it does not speak the complete truth. There are the rapid patter songs to be found in the operettas of Gilbert and Sullivan and there is the rapid syllabizing of buffo passages in Rossini and Donizetti. Both are less sustained than some speech. On the other hand, there are the prolonged vowels associated with certain dialects. We also hear that prolongation of vowels in many calls, such as those used by the baseball umpire. The speaker generally employs a more limited range than the singer, but that too has its exceptions. The range of a song may be very limited and the inflections of a Shakespearian actor or public announcer may be very wide. Nor is it entirely a matter of musical notation, because a speaker too, in a totally unconscious manner, may be employing a pattern of sounds that

85

could be notated. The dictionary in part defines singing as an utterance with musical, melodious sound. This definition fails also because this characteristic is often present in speech. It is difficult to clearly differentiate speech from song, although each of the attempts has contained something that gave an indication of difference. The point that I wish to make is that there is often little difference —**voice is voice.** Those who have developed the singing voice have often had the most beautiful and expressive speaking voices in the world. Those who have fine speaking voices often learn to sing if they develop both registers and have ability to carry a tune.

Development of the speaking voice should be of equal interest to the singer, the actor, the leader, the communicative person. If the speaking voice of the **non-singer** is faulty, that person is handicapped. If the speaking voice of a **singer** is faulty, it will work against the best usage of the singing voice, undermining the foundations of his singing technique.

If you diligently practice and apply the exercises that have been given, you may enhance the beauty of your speaking voice, giving it greater resonance, power, and flexibility. You will be able to use it with more control and to speak with more continuity of sound. You will also find that it will be more closely attuned to your subtlest feelings and that it will be capable of expressing them. If you are musical, you will find that, without aspiring to be a singer, you will develop some ability to sing.

You may have awareness that your speaking voice is ineffective. It may at times seem strained to you. It may become hoarse after prolonged usage. You may realize that people do not give you the attention which you think they should, or that they often ask you to repeat that which you have said. You may suspect that you do not succeed where voice is involved. If you are an actor, you may find that your voice limits the roles which you are able to play, denying those which place great demands upon the voice.

Do not despair if your voice is lacking in quality, power, ease of production, expressiveness; it may be reshaped. However, I must tell you that it will not immediately be done, nor will it be done without effort on your part. You must be motivated by a great desire to possess a fine voice. I assure you that the effort is worthwhile. If your voice is lacking in effectiveness, we must not accept it as the voice given you by nature. We must recognize that there are many unknown factors that have caused your voice to be the voice that it is. We must circumvent the unknown influences. We must replace the old with a new concept of tone.

Even if your voice is ineffective, it probably feels natural to you. It is the voice which you have used day after day for years. But, I must remind you that it is not natural if it is ineffective. To you, the new will be strange. Although we will be striving for nothing more than the natural voice, it will seem unnatural to you. If a man should limp for years, he would have the same experience — walking soundly would seem unnatural. We are supplanting a correct image of tone for an incorrect one. If your speech has not been good, it follows that the transition to the new will cause a feeling of change. The new voice may seem artificial. To use it may for a time bring about self consciousness. Your family, your friends will notice the change. They may approve but they may disapprove, because, at first, your voice will be bound by the technique which you are seeking to make your own. It may seem to them that suddenly you are different from the person they have known for years. A new hair style or a new manner of dress may bring the same reaction, and those things too may be an effort to improve your image and your style of life.

Although the scope of musical pitches is greater in some effective speakers than in others, it is certainly less extensive in speech than in singing. Most speaking occurs within less than half of the range of an operatic singer. It usually takes place within the limits of an octave in the lower part of the voice, sometimes on a very few pitches in the middle of the voice. However, in some foreign languages and English dialects speech is inflected over a much wider range of pitches. Extensive range is also detected in the voices of uninhibited people as well as dramatic actors. One suspects that the usual uninteresting pitch limitation of conversational speech is caused by the shortness of the individual's vocal range. Certainly that person who has extensive range in the voice speaks with a more interesting variation of inflections.

The employment of both registers of the voice is a necessity for expressive singing. It was pointed out in Chapter Five that the coordination between registers in the male voice was in the upper part of the voice. It was also indicated that the coordinated area in the female voice was in the middle of the vocal range. In a sense, this presents a greater problem for male singers, since their much prized upper tones are sung in the coordinated area and the delicate finesse involved in merging the two registers becomes a necessity if they are to possess the full operatic range. A faulty coordination in the female voice may cause a deficiency in the middle of the voice but it is possible that a woman may possess such fine upper tones that the fault is overlooked. However, in speech the problem is somewhat reversed. The coordination is less imperative for men since they generally speak in the low register, but the coordination is a necessity for women if they are to have fine speaking voices. If a woman confines her speaking to the upper register, the voice will be weak and breathy since the upper register by nature is weak and breathy in the range that she will be employing in speech. If she uses only the low register, the voice may be rich and fine but it will be restricted in its range and tend to be strained in the upper parts of the speech patterns. If she is to have an expressive, resonant voice capable of conveying the gamut of emotions and being heard at a distance, she must utilize the low register and the coordinated area between low and high. (See Figure 1).

All of the exercises thus far given for your voice category should help you in the development of your speaking voice. They have been intended to give you the sensations which accompany a correctly produced vocal sound. You must become acutely aware of these sensations, those that are related to the vibration of the tone and those that are related to physical feelings. The physical feelings may have to do with the mouth position, the posterior portion of the tongue, or the feeling at the back of the mouth when you have produced the correct tone. Those sensations will enable you to gain consistency in making the sound and they will enable you to transfer the correct tone to the speaking voice.

The exercises for the development of the separated registers and for the cultivation of a coordination between them must be diligently pursued. Although the cultivation of the upper register and its coordination with the low is not as essential in the development of the male speaking voice, it will enhance the voice. Such a coordination will expand the range, giving greater ease and security when the voice inflects upward. It will also bring beauty and control to the upper pitches of speech.

Women will probably find Exercise 7, (AY, AY, AY) the most helpful in relating the low register to the speaking voice and that should be the first step. Declamatory passages, such as may be found in Shakespeare, will serve well in making the first attempts. However, any reading material may be used if an effort is made to project the voice. Review the exercise and then read the passage with the same kind of tone, with the same sensation. Purposely confine the range to the low register. The speech will be without expression. To make this first step you should concentrate upon nothing other than reproducing the tone. Project the voice as though you were in a large theatre.

Men should reread the instruction for calling the "No" (Exercise 1M). In addition to my remembrance of the vegetable vendor who called "potatoes, tomatoes," related in connection with the called tone, I would like to refer to other calls which are familiar to almost everyone: the prolonged cry of the sailor as he calls "Ship ahoy!" or "Land ho!;" the construction worker's "Take 'er away;" the child who calls "John-ee;" the station master's "All aboard!;" the golfer who yells "Fore!;" the newsboy and his "Extra! Extra! Read all about it!" All of us have heard such sounds. In the narrow passages of the Barrio de

Santa Cruz in Seville I once heard a Spanish junk collector whose *"Comprare una cama"* (I will buy a bed) was a combination of call and chant, one of those declamations which mix song and speech. Avery Robinson arranged a negro convict song, a work song, that utilizes such a call, a call for the "Water Boy." These are sounds that have arisen spontaneously from the impulse to be heard and to be heard through a sound that was produced without strain. They are sounds related to a correct usage of the voice. They will help you learn to use the speaking voice.

Exercise S-1. *Yo-ho!; Hel-lo!; All a-board!; Fore!; Take-'er-away!; John-ee!; Good morn-ing!; Extra! Extra! Read all about it!; Timber!*

These are familiar calls that have already been referred to. They are demonstrated on the tape. You are advised to imitate them, to do them repeatedly. If you associate a different inflection with any of the given calls, try it. The thing to be learned from these spontaneous calls is the feeling of free emission of tone. We withdraw our voices. We must not. We must learn to produce our vocal sounds in a manner that allows them to be easily heard, a production that gives no feeling of strain. When you learn to imitate the sounds and to do them easily you will commence to associate certain sensations with their production. You will probably describe those sensations as others before you have described them. You will probably notice a feeling of vibration or pressure in the forepart of the face, perhaps throughout the upper part of the head. You may be aware of a feeling of openness in that area where mouth joins throat.

You may identify that feeling as your means of experiencing the head vibrations. The exercises are given to help you find those sensations. You must come to know them well since much of your improvement will depend upon your ability to transfer those sensations to speech.

Occupational calls associated with women are less familiar to us. I suppose it is because in past ages women have been less associated than men with outdoor occupations. Some calls such as the "Bossy! Here Bossy!" of a farm girl may relate to speaking but women often call on a very high pitch. We may hear a mother using her high voice to call a child somewhere in the neighborhood. It might be a prolonged "Ma-ry" with the voice inflected upward for an octave or more, the highest pitch well into the upper register, or it might be a downward inflection with the first, or perhaps both syllables in the high register. Imitating such a call is probably of little assistance in relating projection to the speaking voice, since the emphasis is on a pitch far removed from speaking. However, the practice of calling is probably also the best approach for the development of the female voice. As stated earlier, for women the most desirable part of the vocal range for speech is in its lower half. A woman must learn to employ the low register in speaking but she must also develop a coordination between the high and low if her voice is to acquire and retain beauty, power, and expressiveness. In developing that low register and familiarizing yourself with its use, you are advised to practice the calls given in Exercise S-1, but to deliver them principally in the low register. In order to bring that register back to mind, return to the AY, AY, AY of Exercise 7. After making those sounds, try to imitate the calls as delivered by a male voice.

Exercise S-2. *Nyeh!*

Recall the snarl of animals. Discover an easy way of making the tone. You must not feel that it is being forced through the throat. When you have found the comfortable manner of emission it will probably seem to you that the tone buzzes in the front of the face, perhaps on the hard palate above the front teeth, perhaps above that. Pass through the beginning N and prolong the Y and the vowel that follows. Analayze the sensation.

Exercise S-3. *Repeated Wah! Wah! Wah!*

Think of a baby crying. The sound comes out without obstruction. He may do it for long periods of time. He is trying to be heard. He does not become hoarse when he does it. Imitate the sound given on the demonstration record. Make the exercise a part of your routine for voice building.

Exercise S-4. *Glissando on Ah.*

Make an Ah sound on a low pitch of your voice and while prolonging the vowel slide upward in pitch as high as you are comfortably able to do so without changing registers; return to the original pitch, approximately touching all of the intervening pitches. After this concept is established, carry it further by passing over into the upper register. In doing so strive to make imperceptible the passage into the upper voice. This is a difficult skill to acquire. It may try your patience. The exercise is not nonsensical, it is worth learning to do. It will expand your range and make possible wider inflections in your speech. Remember that astonishing acquisitions of skill are possible for a human being; they are being continually exhibited by athletes. This exercise is one of the most important for women who must learn to use the low register in speaking, but must not restrict their speech patterns to the low. The exercise must be practiced. A woman who speaks in the lower pitches will only have a deep voice if she is unable to bridge the registers; she will not be able to find the natural level of the voice, that pitch which is best for the individual, that pitch which easily allows upward and downward inflections.

After proficiency has been achieved in executing the exercises given above, it is time to endeavour to bring to speech the sensations learned from the exercises. Try first with isolated words. Any words will do, but a list which progresses from one syllable to multi-syllable words is given here. Make each word an assignment. Project the words and bring the call sensations into the projection but do not call these words, speak them.

Exercise S-5. *A List of Words to Be Spoken.*

go!	faint	empty
leave!	fame	habit
stay!	jam	yellow
abide	just	lament
best	late	measure
bah!	bellow	northern
blade	correct	realize
yawn	daily	meander
yes	dauntless	cadenza
yeast	daylight	belligerent
yield	emit	barbarous

At first you were given one syllable words in order that you might concentrate on the manner of speaking them and that you might appraise your efforts. You were then given multi-syllable words. The next step is to apply the basic sound, which you are now identifying with certain physical sensations, to groups of words and to sentences. You may find your own but I am also providing a list here.

Exercise S-6. *Sentences to Be Spoken.*
Friends, Romans, countrymen, lend me your ears;
I come to bury Caesar, not to praise him.
　　　　　　　　　　—Shakespeare, *Julius Caesar.*

Arise, arise — My lady sweet, arise!
　　　　　　　　　　—Shakespeare, *Cymbeline.*

Whereat, with blade, with bloody blameful blade,
He bravely broach'd his boiling bloody breast.
　　　　　　　—Shakespeare, *A Midsummer Night's Dream.*

Keeping time, time, time,
In a sort of Runic rhyme,
　　To the throbbing of the bells—
Of the bells, bells, bells,
　　To the sobbing of the bells;
Keeping time, time, time,
　　As he knells, knells, knells,
In a happy Runic rhyme,
　　To the rolling of the bells—
Of the bells, bells, bells,
　　To the tolling of the bells,
Of the bells, bells, bells, bells
　　Bells, bells, bells,—
To the moaning and the groaning of the bells.
　　　　　　　　　　—Poe, *The Bells.*

95

When fishes flew and forests walked
  And figs grew upon thorn,
Some moment when the moon was blood,
  Then surely I was born.
> —Chesterton, *The Donkey.*

Great rats, small rats, lean rats, brawny rats,
Brown rats, black rats, gray rats, tawny rats,
Grave old plodders, gay young friskers . . .
> —Browning, *Pied Piper of Hamelin.*

At midnight, in the month of June,
I stand beneath the mystic moon.
An opiate vapor, dewy, dim,
Exhales from out her golden rim,
And, softly dropping, drop by drop,
Upon the quiet mountain-top,
Steals drowsily and musically
Into the universal valley.
> —Poe, *The Sleeper.*

A savage place; as holy and enchanted
As e'er beneath a waning moon was haunted
By woman wailing for her demon-lover!
> —Coleridge, *Kubla Khan.*

Now you may select reading passages. Excerpts from The Bible, from Shakespeare, from poetry, even from the daily newspaper will provide excellent practice material. At this point we are only referring to technique and the transference of the fundamental sound to speaking. Speech has other aspects which will be briefly discussed, but the principal concern of this book is to direct you to a correct basic manner of producing the tone which you will use in singing or in speaking. The actor with inadequate power and resonance in his voice can never be a versatile actor. The person who would be a leader fails in his ambition if he does not have a command-ing voice. With an inadequate, weak, unauthoritive voice a person projects an image of weakness, of inadequacy; he fails to inspire others to have con-fidence in him. An unpleasant voice turns others away. To gain the technique will require regular practice sessions in which you are doing nothing more than applying to speech the sensations which you have been learning.

Two passages from Shakespeare will be found on the recorded tape (Exercise S-7). They will be read in two ways; first, with concentration on the vocal resonance, with no attention given to expression and, second, with the concentration centered on the meaning behind the lines with little regard to the technique. The tonal play of the first reading will seem ludicrous, it will make no sense; you will hear only illogical inflections and a sustained playing upon the vowels and voiced consonants. Although it may seem ridiculous, it will serve a purpose.

Read the two Shakespearian excerpts and select other passages as well. Explore the full resonance of the voice. Dwell on the vowels and voiced consonants. Experiment with wild inflections. Do anything with your voice that your imagination dictates. Have fun in creating the buzzing resonance, in filling the head with vibrations. Play with the rich musical sound and remember that it will undoubtedly seem very strange to you, perhaps not musical at all. While reading in this manner give attention to the sensa-tions and disregard the strange sounds which you are producing.

Exercise S-7. *Two Excerpts From Shakespeare.*
To be, or not to be; that is the question:
Whether 'tis nobler in the mind to suffer
The slings and arrows of outrageous fortune,
Or to take arms against a sea of troubles,
And, by opposing, end them.—To die, to sleep;
No more: and, by a sleep, to say we end
The heart-ache and the thousand natural shocks
That flesh is heir to—'tis a consummation
Devoutly to be wish'd!—To die, to sleep.
To sleep? perchance to dream! Ay, there's the rub!
For in that sleep of death what dreams may come,
When we have shuffled off this mortal coil,
Must give us pause. There's the respect
That makes calamity of so long life!
For who would bear the whips and scorns of time,
The oppressor's wrong, the proud man's contumely,
The pangs of dispriz'd love, the law's delay,
The insolence of office, and the spurns
That patient merit of the unworthy takes,
When he himself might his quietus make
With a bare bodkin? Who would fardels bear,
To grunt and sweat under a weary life,
But that the dread of something after death,
The undiscover'd country, from whose bourn
No traveller returns, puzzles the will,
And makes us rather bear those ills we have
Than fly to others that we know not of?
Thus conscience does make cowards of us all.
And thus the native hue of resolution
Is sicklied o'er with the pale cast of thought,
And enterprises of great pith and moment,
With this regard; their currents turn awry,
And lose the name of action.
                              —Shakespeare, *Hamlet.*

98

The quality of mercy is not strain'd;
It droppeth as the gentle rain from heaven
Upon the place beneath: it is twice blest;
It blesseth him that gives, and him that takes:
'Tis mightiest in the mightiest: it becomes
The throned monarch better than his crown;
His sceptre shows the force of temporal power,
The attribute to awe and majesty,
Wherein doth sit the dread and fear of kings;
But mercy is above this sceptred sway;
It is enthroned in the hearts of Kings,
It is an attribute to God himself;
And earthly power doth then show likest God's
When mercy seasons justice. Therefore, Jew,
Though justice be thy plea, consider this, —
That, in the course of justice, none of us
Should see salvation: we do pray for mercy;
And that same prayer doth teach us all to render
The deeds of mercy. I have spoke thus much
To mitigate the justice of thy plea;
Which if thou follow, this strict court of Venice
Must needs give sentence 'gainst the merchant there.
—Shakespeare, *The Merchant of Venice.*

It will take time to establish the tonal technique. When you feel that you are being successful in bringing the free resonance into your voice, it is time to think of the ultimate goal in speech—to express yourself. At first it is advisable to alternate between the purely technical approach and expressiveness. Read a passage with no regard to expression, then reread it with an attempt to penetrate and deliver the full meaning, as in the second reading of the passages from Shakespeare. In your endeavour to speak expressively, you will find that you must cease to listen to yourself, to appraise your effort. You must not listen to yourself as you would listen to another. If you do, you will be concentrating upon listening and your speech will be hollow and meaningless. Your concentration must be **completely** upon that which you are saying and the meaning that you are trying to convey. You are no longer the audience listening to the performer — **you** are the performer. Listening to yourself will make you self-conscious and nervous and it will destroy true expression.

Ultimately the voice must be used in the middle of the range of dynamics as well as the middle of the speaking range. You must choose an intensity that may be made louder or softer if expression is to be conveyed. You will learn to accommodate that intensity to your environment. If you are close to a partner in conversation you will match the degree of loudness to the distance involved in communication. However, you must always employ the voice as you have been learning to do; you can then in a moment adjust the volume for greater distances. After the range of the voice has been expanded you must also find the pitch at which you speak most effectively. That pitch will neither be high nor low; it will be somewhere in the middle of the speaking range. It will be placed on such a pitch that the voice is free to move upward and downward with comfort.

The efforts to combine technique with expression may be frustrating. We only hope that the practice which you have applied to the exercises will have sufficiently ingrained the new concept to enable you to retain at least part of it when your concentration is no longer upon it. If it vanishes when you cease to think of it, the technical practice must continue. In the course of time you can make it your own. You will have a voice that will obey the expressive dictates of the mind.

Many people never experience sensations which you are probably by this time associating with your voice. There may be a sense of unreality about your speaking experience. It may seem that the buzzing and rumbling of the resonance which you are creating goes on and on as you speak and that the formation of the words has little to do with the basic continuous sound. You may have awareness that with your mouth and lips and tongue you are articulating syllables as in a dream and that they do nothing more than shape the continuous sound that you make as you speak. It is that continuous sound which we have been trying to achieve. It must be there as a part of the voice. Of course, that unreal part of the voice, the formation of the words is also a necessity. Without clear articulation the sounds convey no specific meaning. That clear articulation is the result of a careful formation of vowels by the tongue, jaw, and lips and consonants by combin-ational uses of the lips, palate, teeth, tongue, vocal cords, and nasal passages. If the basic tone is correct, it will be easier to articulate distinctly. However, fine diction results from at least two things; a precise awareness of how the sounds of speech are made, and from practice in trying to achieve that clear articulation which makes speech a pleasure to hear. To help you become aware of the manner of forming the consonants I will provide brief descriptions of how they are formed. I will also list a few selected words which may be used for regular practice in articulating each of those con-sonants.

CONSONANTS

A consonant is formed by either stopping or impeding the open flow of voice or breath. This may be done by the shaping or closing of lips, by the lower lip in combination with the upper teeth, by the tip of the tongue in contact with the upper teeth, by the tongue in contact with the hard palate or in proximity to the hard palate, by the tongue placed close to or touching the soft palate, by the raising or lowering of the soft palate in combination with tongue or lip action, by the vocal cords partially closing the glottis. Some consonants completely stop the open flow of voice or breath, others only partially impede its flow. Some consonants are produced while the vocal cords are being vibrated; they are called **voiced** consonants. Other consonants are made while the vocal cords are at rest; they are called **voiceless.** The speaker or singer can easily identify this aspect of consonant production by placing the thumb on one side of the larynx and the forefinger on the other side while consonants are being formed (see Figure 27). If a vibration is felt by the fingers, the sound being produced is **voiced.**

The following analyses of consonant formation is presented in categories. These categories have to do with the area of production and the speech organs involved.

GLOTTAL   **H**

H (as in hope, hold)   *Voiceless*

This sound is created by the vocal cords which partially close the glottis, hindering

102

the passage of breath. The position of the tongue which is already placed for the following vowel also contributes to the aspirate sound.

Words to be practiced:

hat	heal	withhold
hand	height	hard-hearted
hail	helm	cohort
had	hem	unheard
haze	him	unhurt

Misuse:
In some accents (such as cockney) the H is not pronounced when it should be and added where it should not be present. Examples: *'ead* for *head* and *hexamine* for *examine.*

SOFT PALATE—BACK OF TONGUE   K,G,NG.

G (as in gone)   *Voiced*
The sound produced by the vocal cords is momentarily stopped by the back of the tongue which rises to touch the soft palate.

Words to be practiced:

gag	grit	ingoing
gage	goon	mitigate
go	giggle	Hungary
gift	doggy	prognostic
grave	ingrain	ingratitude

K (as in king)   *Voiceless*

This sound is the voiceless counterpart of G (gone). Only the breath is stopped by the tongue action, since the vocal cords are not vibrating.

Words to be practiced:

kill	corn	thick
kind	cab	factory
kit	came	pluck
kale	caldron	jocular
koala	canteen	hook

NG (as in sing)   *Voiced*

The back of the tongue is raised to the soft palate which is lowered, allowing the vocalized sound to resonate in the nasal passages.

Words to be practiced:

king	rank	dancing
bring	stinger	blessing
sung	whining	winging
long	clanging	wronging
cling	singing	haranguing

Words in which a G is sounded following the NG

language	manganese	finger
languorous	mangle	hunger

Caution!
Do not conclude a final NG with an added G or K, as singing-k or clanging-g. Be sure

that you pronounce final NG distinctly. Do not say singin' for singing.

HARD PALATE—TONGUE   Y, H (as in hue)

Y (as in yes)   *Voiced*

The tongue, down in front, is arched so that it almost touches the hard palate. It impedes the vocalized sound.

Words to be practiced:

yet	yearn	cute
yell	brilliant	cue
yield	million	young
yeoman	feud	youth
yellow	yawn	union

H (as in hue)   *Voiceless*

This sound is the voiceless cognate of Y. The tongue is placed as it is for Y. The breath is hissed between the tongue and the hard palate.

Words to be practiced:

hew	humorous
human	humility
humidity	inhumane

TEETH RIDGE—TONGUE   D,T,N,Z,S,ZH,SH,L,R

These consonants are often faintly pronounced or mispronounced. They are a part of the largest category of consonants. They should be practiced assiduously.

D (as in dot)   *Voiced*

The soft palate is raised, the tip of the tongue is pressed firmly against the teeth ridge and a voiced sound is made as the tongue is drawn away from the teeth ridge.

Words to be practiced:

dill	edit	hound
din	raid	sudden
do	doodle	predicate
drift	deacon	elucidate
drawl	middle	punctuated

To avoid:

Often the D is made with the full tongue in a semi-relaxed position touching a large part of the hard palate. The result is a thick, dull, indistinct sound. Practice placing the tip of the tongue slightly behind the front teeth and the sound produced will be clean and distinct.

T (as in time)   *Voiceless*

This consonant is the voiceless counterpart of D. The tip of the tongue is pressed against the teeth ridge and drawn quickly away while breath is expelled.

Words to be practiced:

tell	twice	telltale
tick	total	teletype
test	totter	transmit
tip	teapot	teetotaler
talk	cotton	transcendent

To avoid:
Be sure that you do not substitute D for T, lidl for little. Also avoid the thick tongue pronunciation described above under D. Practice articulating the sound cleanly with the tip of the tongue.

N (as in note)   *Voiced*
A voiced sound is made through the nose, while the tip and edges of the tongue are pressed against the upper teeth ridge and the soft palate is lowered to open the nasal passages.

Words to be practiced:

none	name	antagonist
onset	inane	ordination
never	taken	anonymous
knell	anoint	omnipotent
gnaw	silken	nothing

To strive for:
If the tip of the tongue is raised to the teeth ridge instead of a large part of the front of the tongue a cleaner articulation will result, giving greater purity to adjacent vowels.

Z (as in zero)   *Voiced*
The jaw is almost closed. The sides of the tongue touch the sides of the gums. The tip of the tongue is placed close to the front teeth ridge. The vocal cords are vibrated while the escaping breath hisses lightly through the grooved position of the tongue. This is called a sibilant sound.

Words to be practiced:

zing	buzzing	xenophobia
zest	confusing	zepplin
zephyr	drizzle	zodiac
zebra	advertise	zoology
zone	energize	exercise

S (as in sea) *Voiceless*

The voiceless counterpart of Z. This consonant is produced as the Z but without vocal cord action. It is referred to as a sibilant.

Words to be practiced:

simple	synthesize	plastic
silk	hacienda	monastic
sent	hyacinth	handsome
sought	symbolist	simplistic
said	studious	thistle

Give attention!

Since the S can be an unappealing sound, care must be taken in its pronunciation. It must be pronounced distinctly but not too forcefully. After a voiced consonant at the end of a word it should be pronounced as Z. If the tongue touches the front teeth, a lisp will result.

ZH (as in azure) *Voiced*

As in other sibilants the jaw is almost closed. The body of the tongue is raised toward the roof of the mouth and held firmly in place. The tip of the tongue is close to the front teeth ridge. The vocal cords are vibrated and the escaping breath is hissed between the front of the tongue and the front teeth ridge.

Words to be practiced:

treasure	rouge	illusion
pleasure	corsage	usury
azure	massage	vision
profusion	mirage	measure
infusion	garage	conclusion

Take care!
If the tongue is not pressed firmly the sound will become unpleasant. If it is not firmly vocalized, it will emerge as a kind of SH. If the tongue touches the front teeth it will be objectionably sibilant.

SH (as in shell)   *Voiceless*

This is the voiceless counterpart of ZH, produced in the same manner but without vibration of the vocal cords.

Words to be practiced:

short	swish	shuttle
shy	nation	shoestring
shame	shrieks	admission
shall	fishing	permission
shun	shyster	shortsighted

L (as in lilt)   Voiced

The tip of the tongue is pressed against the teeth ridge, close to the back of the front teeth. The soft palate is raised and the vocal cords are vibrated.

Words to be practiced:

lad	malinger	little
lain	lateral	please
late	ladylove	Longfellow
limp	lollipop	candlelight
lazy	mallet	longitudinal

For a better sound:
Keep the tongue forward as for the D and T; it may even touch the front teeth near the gum line. If it does, the sound will be cleaner.

R (as in run)   *Voiced*
The sound is made with the tip of the tongue raised toward the hard palate, preferably forward toward the front teeth ridge. The vocal cords are vibrated and the tone is restricted in its passage between the tongue and palate.

Caution!
This is a consonant which requires much care in its production. It is ugly in sound when it is prolonged, and, since the vocal cords are being vibrated during its production, it is possible to prolong it. If the tip of the tongue is turned backward, an inverted R is created. This sound, which has been particularly characteristic of the western part of the United States, may be very undesirable. In good speech it is handled very lightly at the ends of words. In some of the best of English speech it is entirely dropped at the ends of words. When it occurs be-

tween vowels it may be flapped once very delicately, this too is very often heard in England. Those who have been accustomed to making an inverted R sound have difficulty in determining the vowel of the syllable which is terminated by the R. The speaker or singer must learn to know the vowel of that syllable, giving the prolongation to it, rather than to the R. He must speak the vowel clearly, avoiding one that is mixed with the R.

Words to be practiced:

red	artful	purse
three	artery	never
Mary	quarrel	fatter
father	try	irreverent
farthing	very	better

J (as in just)   *Voiced*

This sound is actually a combination of two tongue-teeth ridge consonants. It begins with D, and as the voiced sound is made it progresses to ZH.

Words to be practiced:

judge	jelly	plumage
educate	jeer	partridge
adjudicate	ageless	porridge
ajoin	project	January
agent	jump	gypsy

CH (as in chime)   *Voiceless*

This is the voiceless cognate of ZH. It is actually a combination of T and SH, both of

111

which have been described. The tongue is placed in the position to make a T but after the beginning of the sound it is lowered to the SH position.

Words to be practiced:

cheek	cherry	pitch
chin	chimney	richest
chubby	chiffchaff	peaches
chop	checkmate	poaching
chive	question	vulture

Caution!

The sound should be sharply made at the end of a word, taking care that the SH is not prolonged. In such words as *richest* or *poaching* make certain that the T part of the combined sound is pronounced, it is often omitted.

TONGUE—TEETH CONSONANTS   **TH**

TH (as in then)   *Voiced*

The tip of the tongue touches the back of the front teeth, or it touches the bottom of the front teeth while the vocal cords are vibrated. The obstruction of the tongue creates a fricative sound.

Words to be practiced:

thou	bathing	thine
they	clothing	heather
them	breathe	leather
there	smooth	either
thus	unworthy	blather

Two mistakes:

Some foreigners substitute D for the proper sound. Even some dialects in America are guilty of pronouncing *dis* for *this, der* for *there.*

If the tongue is pressed too firmly against the front teeth, the tone is stopped. The pressure against the teeth is a light one, allowing the sound to pass between the teeth and the tongue.

TH (as in thin)   *Voiceless*

This sound is the voiceless counterpart of the TH in then which has just been described.

Words to be practiced:

thick	with	faithful
thermal	width	thunder
thievery	thistle	pathway
think	breadth	hundredth
third	theatre	withstanding

A fault:

A common fault is the failure to pronounce this consonant distinctly. In words like *thousandths* the sound is difficult to pronounce and consequently often omitted.

LIP-TEETH CONSONANTS   V,F

V (as in very)   *Voiced*

The lips are slightly raised, the lower lip touching the front teeth and pressing against them. The vocal cords are vibrated as the sound is made, but the characteristic fricative sound comes from the breath passing between the lip and teeth.

Words to be practiced:

vile	victor	envious
give	volley	vertebra
prove	vibrate	invocation
view	believe	vilification
vital	vintage	vernacular

Possible mistakes:

If the lips are touching each other when the sound is made, something of a B will result. If the lips are pursed to too great an extent, the sound may be confused with WH (when). Pronounce the consonant distinctly, sometimes it is omitted or sounded so lightly that it does not project.

F (as in funny)   *Voiceless*

This is the voiceless cognate of V. The vocal cords are not vibrated during its production. Otherwise it is made as the V.

Words to be practiced:

fail	fortitude	nephew
fate	clef	laugh
fan	enough	flavorful
force	fitful	philosophy
fin	dreadful	deftness

Possible mistakes:
If the lower lip is protruded and not held sufficiently by the teeth, the sound may resemble P. If the vocal cords are vibrated when the sound is being made, it will emerge as V. Sometimes it is sounded so weakly that it is inaudible. Sound it distinctly.

LIP CONSONANTS   **B,P,M,W**

B (as in boat)   *Voiced*
The lips are pressed firmly together; a voiced sound is made; and the lips are parted. The pressure of the pent-up voiced breath allowed to suddenly escape with the parting of the lips creates a plosive sound. When the B is used at the ends of words the lips usually remain closed, thus eliminating the plosion. Description of this consonant is made difficult by the variety of subtle ways in which it is used. When followed by an L the tongue is in place for the L formation when the lips are closed for the B. In this manner the B plosion is minimized and the sounds are made almost simultaneously. When the B is followed by another B,

115

or another plosive such as D,T,K, the lips remain compressed for a slightly longer period of time and the plosion or release of air occurs on the following consonant. This occurs in words such as *robbed, bobtail.*

Words to be practiced:

bin	rob	bibliography
bat	knob	bobtail
boat	bobby	sobbed
bright	babble	bobolink
bowl	cabin	bloody

Take care:
The vocal cords must vibrate to produce the sound. If they do not, a P will be the result. Carefully differentiate this sound from W or V by pressing the lips firmly together.

P (as in pan)   *Voiceless*

This consonant is the voiceless counterpart of B. The sound is created by the sudden release of breath as the lips part. The pressure which creates the lightly plosive sound is made possible by the soft palate automatically closing off the nasal passage, thereby preventing the breath from going through the nose. This palate action is also present in the production of B.

Words to be practiced:

put	popping	caption
pen	platter	napkin
pleated	peep	pippin
pool	captivate	hope

116

Be sure:

Produce the sound distinctly. Press the lips firmly together and part them quickly. If they are not pressed firmly, the sound may be confused with F. If the sound is produced while the vocal cords vibrate, it will not be distinguished from B.

M (as in mine)   *Voiced*

The vocal cords are vibrated, the lips are pressed together, the soft palate is lowered to allow the sound to pass through the nasal passages.

Words to be practiced:

man	him	mimic
maid	seem	moonlight
mean	clam	mammoth
mint	tram	momentum
moose	bomb	memorandum

W (as in with)   *Voiced*

The lips are tightly pursed, forward, and away from the teeth. The rounded opening of the lips is similar to the position for whistling. The sound may be prolonged, since the vocal cords are vibrated and the sound is not totally interrupted by the lips.

Words to be practiced:

wind	once	bewitched
woman	sweet	woodwork
weep	twitter	Wedgwood
wound	unwound	Wordsworth
wail	werewolf	workwoman

WH (as in whistle)   *Voiceless*

This sound is the voiceless counterpart of W. The lips are pursed in the same way. As the sound is terminating, they move toward the position of the following vowel.

Words to be practiced:

when	whistle	nowhere
what	whither	meanwhile
where	whittle	whimper
white	whisk	whine
whip	whippet	wheel

VOWELS

I do not propose in this book to speak in detail concerning the formation of vowels. They are formed by adjustments in the size or shape of the resonance chambers of the voice. For the English vowels these adjustments are made by reducing or enlarging the oral cavity through a lowering or partial closing of the jaw, by a raising or lowering of the tongue, or by a shaping of the lips. Instruction concerning the formation of vowels has often been nothing more than a description of that which usually occurs when people produce a particular vowel. I have already discussed the prevalence of poor voice production. This poor production is, of course, apparent in vowels which are the substance of vocal tone. I have tried to present a manner of producing tone correctly. That manner of natural voice production brings about a lowered position of the back of the tongue. It is imperative that that position be approximately retained during all vowel production. It is possible to produce all vowels with that position and that means that the reductions in the size of the oral resonance chamber will be brought about by a partial closing of the jaw and a slight raising of the forepart of the tongue in the production of EE and IH (as in it). Shape the lips to form vowels, close the jaw to form closed vowels, but do not lose the sensations which you have identified with the correctly produced tone.

8

Applying the Sounds to Singing

You are more likely to have been successful with these sounds if you have considered them unrelated to singing. Thinking of them in this way will help you by-pass misconceptions and more directly regain the natural voice.

When you find the natural voice, you will have found the means of acquiring the great singing voice. It is often said that the voice of the skilled singer has been given to him as a divine gift, that he has been born with that voice. In my opinion such a singer has only been fortunate enough to have used his voice in a correct manner and while doing so has developed unusual strength and skill in its use. Through such sounds as those given in these exercises, it is possible for you also to acquire a great voice.

The sounds which have been demonstrated are directly related to singing. If you make these sounds your own, apply them to music, give feeling and sensitivity to that music, sing with an expressiveness that arises from human emotions, you will have done something which is beautiful. The tone of the great singer has a basic resemblance to the kind of sound that has been given to you in the recorded exercises. It is the mind and heart of man which makes such tones expressively beautiful. Though it may cause you to smile, can you not see that the rich fine tone of the cow would be an admirable one for singing if that beast had music in its ears and human emotions in its heart? Let the natural voice rule! Cultivate it until it is once again a part of you. Add concentration, the desire to be expressive, and imagination to that natural tone and you will find that it will be responsive to your expressive desires. It will even convey something more than words can express.

The only unnatural thing about singing is the application of the natural voice to long and complex melodies with words. Such melodies are probably the outgrowth of natural human inflections but they are more involved than the usual human utterance.

If you have gained fair consistency in producing the exercise sounds correctly, you are ready to take the initial steps in applying that natural tone to singing. The first efforts to sing with that kind of tone will require intense concentration.

A song should now be selected so that an attempt may be made. That song should be of moderate or slow tempo to enable you to concentrate on the kind of sound which you will attempt to apply. The song should not be musically difficult; your concentrated effort to apply the newly found tone to actual singing must not be diffused by musical difficulties. The song should not be of extensive range. For women the high tone should be only slightly lower than the pitch on which the singer is comfortably calling the "Hoo-ee." For men the high tone of the song should probably be a full tone lower than the tone on which the singer is easily sounding the called "No."

Try now to dismiss from your mind all previous thoughts regarding singing and sing this song with the kind of tone which you have been using in the exercises. Remember the feeling which those exercises have given you and the sound which you heard when you made them. Try, above all else, to sing with that same kind of tone. Little attention can, at first, be given to interpretation, to diction, or to dynamics. Your beginning efforts may seem awkward. They will seem awkward because no thought is being given to the finesse of singing and because the tone may be very different from that which you have used before. Yet, it is likely that, even in this beginning effort, you will achieve some success. If you have previously sung with a different kind of tone, the sound which you will now apply will undoubtedly be a strange one to your own ears. It will seem very loud to your associates unless they have experienced the bigness of fine voices.

At this point you are very much in need of the assistance of one who understands what you are trying to do and who is capable of appraising your effort. If you do not have someone who is capable of recognizing correctness or incorrectness in this basic but perhaps unrefined sound, you must depend upon your own judgement and recordings of your voice. You are probably on the path of improvement if you feel greater freedom in your singing; if the tone comes out with a buzzing, ringing resonance; if it seems to you that you are producing the sound as you have produced it in the exercises.

In your first attempts to apply the technique to song, you will probably notice that you are more successful with certain sounds than with others.

Perhaps there is a higher tone which comes out with more freedom than the others. Perhaps there is a vowel that is produced more easily than the others. You should not be greatly concerned, at first, about a vowel or a high or low tone which is troublesome. You are trying to establish a concept of the kind of tone which should be applied. You will learn to apply it to all vowels throughout an extensive range of your voice when that concept is established in your mind through the exercises, and when you have associated certain physical sensations with that kind of tone. We improve by doing a thing in the right manner. If you attempt to immediately solve the problem of an incorrectly produced vowel by drilling that particular sound you will repeatedly be doing something that is wrong. Simply continue the exercises and keep trying to apply the concept to your singing. Remember this, in establishing the voice it is better to drill that thing which we perform easily and correctly than to drill the thing which is difficult and incorrect.

You may feel encouraged if to any degree you have been successful in employing the tone in your singing. If you have been, it is because you have a better understanding of how you should sing. The success in employing the tone, even though it may be slight, will have given you still more understanding. With this knowledge you are certainly in a position to bring about a great improvement to your voice.

Learning to sing with the newly found tone will require patience and perseverance. Consider the song an exercise in which you are only striving to apply the natural sound to singing. Return to your exercises intermittently while making the efforts to apply the sound. Our memories are short; it is difficult to retain a clear remembrance of the model tone. The exercises must be repeated in order to freshen the memory. When you feel that you are calling the tones freely and clearly, the first phrase of the song should again be tried. Ask yourself if the tone is identical to the tone made in the exercise. Does it have the same freedom? Give little concern to the interpretation of the song in the early stage although that should be your principal concern after the technique has been established. Concentrate upon the tone and stop if you feel that it is slipping away. Return to the exercises and try again. If you are endeavoring to establish correct habits of singing, you must not relapse into former incorrectness. Avoid attacks which slide upward until the pitch is met; avoid an easing into the tone. Try to recollect the sound before you produce it and then attack the note quickly and directly before old habits take over. If the inhaling sound gives evidence of being useful, that is, if the tone comes out more clearly and securely after using it, do not hesitate to employ the exercise with frequency, even stopping before phrases or before a high tone to make that sound. Eventually it will have served its purpose; you will be able to find the proper throat position without it, or by merely thinking the sound.

Men may find that calling the words of the song, as demonstrated on the recording (Exercise S-5), will be helpful in transferring the natural sound to actual singing, but it is not advisable for women to do so.

Proceed with the song, trying again and again, using your own inventiveness but always striving for an exact transference of the sound and feeling which you have learned.

I do not intend to imply that this manner of learning to use the voice is a shortcut, an easy means of acquiring an art. There are no shortcuts to art or to the acquisition of a skill. Such things are attained only through perseverance. There is such a thing, however, as directness in teaching. If a student is put upon the right path, he may with persistence achieve his ambition to sing. If directions are vague and the student fails to find the way, he may work and work and eventually learn that his work has been unavailing, that he can never reach his destination.

9
Make Those Registers Work As One

Effective performance of most songs written for women necessitates the employment of both registers. If a woman is utilizing the full potential of her voice, the singing of any note as low as D^4 and as strong as *mezzo forte* necessitates the use of the low register, while any note as high as F^5 requires that the upper register be used. (See Figure 1, page 58.)

Seldom, however, do the songs performed by male singers of the present day necessitate the use of an unadulterated high register. Abnormal emphasis of the low register has increased since the middle of the nineteenth century. Operatic composers during the early part of that century wrote many notes for the tenor voice which could only have been sung by a singer whose upper register was greatly developed.

The tenor role of Arnold in Rossini's Guillaume Tell, for example, requires, even in modern scores, 456 Gs, 93 A flats, 54 B flats, 15 Bs, 19 Cs and 2 C sharps! Nor does the role avoid low tones; the lowest B flat in the tenor voice appears twelve times. Rossini actually gave the tenor more high tones than this to sing. In a nineteenth century score I counted 52 high Cs, 3 C sharps, 2 Ds and 1 E flat. The part was written for Adolphe Nourrit (1802-1839) who also premiered the title role in Rossini's Le Comte Ory and Raoul in Meyerbeer's Les Huguenots. Nourrit reigned supreme with his superb acting, sensitive singing, and spendorous voice until Gilbert Duprez appeared upon the operatic scene and hurled out stentorian high Cs "from the chest." Rossini intensely disliked the high tone of Duprez, likening it to "the squawk of a capon having its throat cut." However, the climactic tones of Duprez so captivated the public fancy that it quite revolutionized the style of operatic writing and dethroned Nourrit as the reigning operatic favorite.[1]

The vocal score of Bellini's I Puritani included an F above high C which the composer inserted for the famous tenor Rubini. It is said that Bellini wrote D in the score, but Rubini, in reading through the role, sang F by mistake. Whereupon, Bellini, learning that Rubini could easily sing the F, inserted it in the score.

Even Donizetti's well known opera Lucia di Lammermoor contains an E flat above high C which present day tenors customarily must omit because of their preponderant emphasis of the low register. Edgardo in Lucia was first sung by barrel-chested Duprez who drove Nourrit from the stage. Even Duprez must have used more of the upper register than the dramatic tenors of our century.

A general acceptance of male high register quality by the audiences of that epoch surely was responsible for its employment. Since it is apparent that the upper register was freely used and developed, it is almost certain that the singers of the period brought more of that register into the blend between

---

[1]Despondent from the loss of favor which he experienced, Nourrit hurled himself to his death from a hotel window in Naples on March 9, 1839.

the two registers than the male vocalists of the present day who rarely develop the high register sufficiently, and who place too great an emphasis upon the low. Only a highly developed coordination between the two registers and a willingness to let the upper register do its part could explain the tenor's ability to sing a tessitura such as that of Arnold in Guillaume Tell.

Although a man, in the current fashion of singing, is rarely required to sing in the pure high register, it is absolutely necessary that he develop that register. Without it he cannot acquire fine upper tones, ease of voice production, and control of intensity. The high tones which he will be required to sing will necessitate a coordination of the low register muscles and those which carry the burden of tension in producing the high register. This coordination will also be of great importance in graduations of loudness and softness above the middle of the voice. The word coordination implies that two things are present. The two necessary things in these aspects of voice production are low and high register. A man has usually neglected the high register. He must cease to neglect it. Furthermore, he must develop strength in it which has been lost through neglect.

The following exercises and discussion, intended to assist in achieving a blend between the registers, are presented separately for men and women because of the range difference in their voices.

Exercises for the Blending of Registers in the Female Voice

Probably the greatest step toward achieving a blend between the registers is simply the employment of both registers in singing. The desired coordination will not immediately take place but, in most instances, it will develop over a period of time. It is important, therefore, that women commence as soon as possible to use both registers in their singing.

If you are one who has not been accustomed to using both registers, it will be necessary to make some conscious effort to do so. Select a song which may be used for the first experiments in this undertaking. In making your first attempts to employ both registers, you will find that intervals which plunge in and out of the low register, skipping the bridge of difficult notes, will at first be much easier to negotiate than scale passages. The transition in moderately loud singing usually takes place between E^4 flat and G^4 in women's voices. A sustained melody which occasionally drops below E flat, but for the most part lies above F sharp, will probably be the best choice for beginning experimentation in the use of registers. Ability to smoothly handle scale passages through the register bridge will probably only be acquired after practicing for a considerable period of time.

If the low register has never before been used, it will seem very strange to employ it. You will have to make a determined effort to draw it into your singing, arbitrarily establishing a pitch on which you will shift over into that register. At first the change should be made on C sharp or D, later this changing point may be raised to E flat or, in occasional instances, to slightly higher pitches. It will be advisable in practicing a song to pause intermittently and repeat Exercise 7 before singing a pitch which should be rendered in the low register. This will bring the sound back into your mind and better enable you to pass completely into that register when you sing the note. The quality of this part of the voice will probably seem exceedingly coarse and unpleasant if you have not used it before. There will be some awkwardness in handling it and the change from low to high, or vice versa, will be far more noticeable to you than to any other listener. The shift from one register to the other will probably seem as deliberate as the shifting of gears in driving a gear shift automobile. It may seem that you are yodeling, breaking from one register to the other. If you are unaccustomed to using the low register you must remember that a coordination will not immediately take place.

Exercise 8 *Two Octave Descending Scale*

Use the vowel OO for this exercise. Attack the high tone with the same sound that you have employed for the Hoo-ee (Exercise 1). Sing the scale as it descends for two octaves. When the second octave is approached, endeavor to bring some low register into the tone. You should strive for a smooth passage from high to low and you should be certain that the last few tones of the scale have been sung entirely in the low register. You may begin on various pitches, providing that the scale allows you to involve both registers.

131

Exercise 9 *Nine Tone Scale.*

AY-OO

The vowel AH is suggested. Sing the lowest note of the scale in your low register. Lighten the voice as it passes to the higher pitches, allowing coordination with the upper register. Be certain that you are not experiencing sprain caused by carrying too much of the low register into the upper notes of the scale. Strive for smoothness. Eliminate the break between registers. Do not force the voice. Sing with only a moderate amount of volume until smoothness is achieved. In descending from the highest note, endeavor to press the voice gently toward the low register, entering it without a perceptible break. Be certain that you have arrived solidly in the low register when the lowest note is reached.

Exercise 10 *AY-OO on Tonic-Dominant Arpeggio*

AY-OO

Sing the first note on AY and immediately change to the vowel OO. It is essential that the OO be produced correctly and for that reason I give the following advice concerning the formation of an OO.

The OO Vowel

The vowel OO, which is employed for most of these exercises, will be very helpful in developing coordination between the registers. You should give no special attention to the formation of this vowel when practicing in the high register. However, it is frequently necessary to give careful attention to its formation in the low register, particularly to the manner of closing the mouth. The mouth should be well opened to produce the AH but nearly closed to shape the OO. That vowel necessitates a reduction in the size of that resonance chamber. The resonance chambers of the voice are the throat, the mouth, the naso-pharynx, the lungs and the sinuses. The throat must remain open for all well produced vowels. The lungs have no power to alter a vowel. The sinuses are not changeable in shape. Minor alteration of the size and shape of the nasopharynx by means of the palate does not form a vowel sound, although it may be used for nasalization, as in certain French vowels. The necessary reduction of the resonance chamber for the formation of the OO must be made by the mouth. The jaw and the tongue are the means of reducing the size of the oral cavity. If the jaw fails to close as the OO is being shaped, the tongue will rise in the back to bring about the reduction in the size of the mouth cavity. The tongue must not rise if the tone is to be clear and resonant. In forming the OO the tongue should remain in the same flat position which it assumes for the production of a ringing AH. If the jaw does not close normally and rapidly when the vowel is changed to OO, the lips, as well as the tongue, will attempt to compensate for the open position. Stretched tightly over the teeth, the unnatural closure of the lips will cause a hollow-

133

ness of sound. In order to avoid this incorrect action of the tongue and lips, you must be certain that the jaw movement begins simultaneously with the impulse to change to the OO. You must also be certain that the jaws come closely together. Only after the upper and lower molars are practically touching should the lips be rounded and thrust slightly forward to complete the formation of the OO.

If you have been successful in obtaining the desired sound on the initial tone of the scale, you may assume that the throat is in the correct position for singing. In singing the arpeggio you must make every possible effort to retain that position. The low register will surrender to the high during the execution of the exercise, but you will probably be more successful in bringing about a coordination between the two registers if you do not try to shift to the high. The first attempts are almost certain to be devoid of smoothness. However, it is also almost certain that the break between registers will not be as noticeable to others as it is to you. You must not be discouraged if you are unable to immediately accomplish your aim; it may take much practicing over an extended period of time.

Exercises for the Blending of Registers in the Male Voice

Exercise 4M. *Two Octave Descending Scale*

    The high tone should be attacked with full voice in the high register. Return to Exercise 3M to remind yourself of the sound and feeling of the completely released upper register. The first tone of this exercise must be identical to that called tone. The descent into the low register should be executed smoothly and an effort must be made to press some of the low register into the tone as soon as possible. At the beginning you may descend to the first F before employing any low register but soon you should bring the coordination into notes higher than that.

    It is not essential that the scale begin on the high C indicated in the notation of the exercise. It would be well to begin on the best upper register tone that you are able to produce and that may be higher or lower than C.

Exercise 5M. *Nine Tone Scale.*

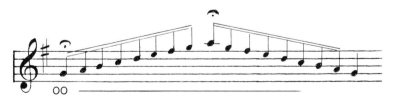

Begin with a soft but resonant OO. At the beginning I would advise that you sustain the initial tone long enough to listen to it and to feel the vibrations. I am hopeful that you will be able to feel vibrations in the head and that it will sound somewhat like a hum. Do not make a loud sound. That will cause you to carry the low register higher than we desire for this exercise and will make it more difficult to pass smoothly into the high register.

Now, while retaining the OO sound, sing the complete scale, allowing the voice to pass completely from one register to the other. It is possible that you can sing the scale without going into the pure upper register but at first we do not want the exercise done in that manner. With this assignment you are training yourself to go from one register to the other and to negotiate the passage with smoothness. If you are able to do that smoothly, you will have sung several notes with a coordination between those muscles principally involved with the low register and those principally involved with the high. If you later develop such extraordinary coordination of the registers that you are able to sing the scale easily without losing something of the low register in the highest pitches, I would recommend that you spend periods of time practicing in that way but that you always alternate these sessions with the practice of intentionally passing into the high register. A singer must not lose the ability to completely separate the registers.

Exercise 6M. *"No" on a Descending Arpeggio.*

NO NO NO   NO NO NO NO NO   NO NO NO NO

Before doing this exercise call out the "No" of Exercise 1 M in order to recall that sound. Endeavor to sing this exercise with exactly the kind of tone used for the called "No."

There is usually an inclination to employ too much of the low register in the higher tones if scales or arpeggios are approached from the lower tones. Caution must be taken to emphasize high register in the upper part of the range. We, therefore, approach this exercise from the highest note of the arpeggio. By such drill we encourage the muscles of the high register to do their part in carrying the tension and that results in a greater beauty of tone and an easier manner of production. To further encourage this it is helpful to occasionally precede the loud "No" of the arpeggio with the very soft one also demonstrated as part of this exercise. In practical application, that is, in the singing of songs, the singer most frequently approaches the high tone from one that is lower. These exercises are intended to help you develop a technique of vocal production. When that technique is established, you will find no difficulty in approaching the high tone from those that are lower and in singing it with ease.

Exercise 7M. *An Octave Skip on "AH."*

Men who have learned to sing fine high tones often remember an early experience associated with that learning. In describing their discovery of those tones, they may say something like this: "I felt the tone flip over and into place. After that I knew how to do it." What are they trying to describe? Before that discovery they had not learned, as the voice went higher, to transfer the tension of the low register muscles to those muscles involved with production of the high. They were trying to sing high tones with the low register and had not yet learned that delicate maneuver which takes place in coordinating the two registers. Suddenly they had discovered how to make use of the high register; they released the tension of the low and probably found a synergetic working of the muscles of both registers. It was a new sensation. It felt as though the voice lifted over toward the high register. It seemed that the tone had flipped into place. The discovery was a very important one. The tone which had been discovered was probably not perfect, but it was one that very likely continued to grow, to improve, and to spread its influence throughout the upper range of the voice.

There is a particular quality that is noticeable when the greatest of male singers produce tones in the upper fourth of their singing range. This characteristic quality has sometimes been a source of wonderment. Some have referred to it as the "covered" tone, as contrasted with the blatant "open" quality which is often heard. I have avoided the use of these terms because I feel that, like many other descriptions, they lead to confusion. A singer often interprets a "covered" tone as one that is smothered. If the singer does not understand the cause of this particular quality but recognizes that it is a part of a great voice, he may try to cultivate it in an improper manner. What **is** the cause of this particular tone color? It is the sound which we as listeners detect in that singer who is feeling the passing over of the low register into the coordinated area.

Teachers have often tried to cultivate a throat position which allows passage into the upper tones. I am not in disagreement with this, but I believe that the throat position which allows passage into the high register is a throat position which should always be present in the voice. I believe that that position has to do with the placement of the back of the tongue and that will be described in a later chapter. I think that that tongue position is usually acquired by proceeding as we have in our quest for the natural tone and that it is not a thing to be artificially cultivated, except in rare cases. I also believe that the most important preparation for learning to sing the high tones has already been given to you in those exercises which have to do with developing the high register and then cultivating a coordination between the two. If that coordination is developed, you will understand the sensation which the great singer discovers in learning to produce fine tones in the higher pitches and you yourself are almost certain to acquire the ability to produce such tones in that area of the voice.

Even though the singer may have developed strength in the high register and some smoothness in singing the scales which pass from one register to the other, he may still find it necessary to learn to handle the registers in actual singing. It will probably be rather easy to completely change registers, to leave the low and pass entirely into the high. This is a part of singing which, if handled skillfully, may produce beautiful and expressive effects. However, that is a skill which is limited in its usefulness and cannot substitute for the ringing voluminous sounds which are often required for climaxes in the upper range of the voice. Even if some coordination is present, the singer may still find some difficulty in acquiring the feeling associated with such tones. Often it is not discovered in the lowest part of the coordinated area but in the upper part. Since the singer may have difficulties with pitches above F, it may seem that a high B or C is an impossibility. It may not be. If the high register has been strengthened as we have been proposing through such an exercise as 3M, the singer may discover a fine high C before he has solved the difficulties of the transition lower in the coordinated area. If he has the good fortune to make such a discovery, he will become acquainted with a sensation which will be of immense help in solving problems several notes below that pitch. It is often thought that high tone problems must be solved step by step and that the range will gradually be extended upward. That has not been my experience. It has become apparent that in many cases the problems in the lower part of the transition cannot be solved until the singer has become familiar with the sensation associated with the highest tones in the coordinated area. When he knows that sensation, he approaches the problem from above, rather than from below. He seeks to find the same sensation lower in the transition; he strives for the same feeling throughout the entire register bridge. It is with the hope of making such a discovery that this exercise is provided. It should not be undertaken until the singer commands the separated high register (Exercise 3M) and has developed strength in its production.

The exercise is performed with an upward skip

of an octave. Begin with a solid resonant sound and follow it with a full voiced tone an octave above. If you are successful, you will probably experience the "flip" or "lift over" toward the upper voice, but it will seem different than the *Hoo-ee* has felt. A greater brilliance of tone will be present. The sound may seem strange, but it will be easily produced. It will be so easily produced that it will seem incredible to you that you have made a good tone. Even if the tone which you have made is exceptionally good, it will sound strange to you. Do not dismiss it until someone experienced in hearing good vocal tones has appraised it, or until you have heard it recorded. The full voiced high C sounds to another as an extension of the low register. It is not; it is somewhere between the two separated registers, but more related to the upper than to the low. Our sights are lofty! We are striving for a high tone that is the prize of some of the world's great singers; we are striving for a tone which is even beyond the skill of some of the great male singers. It should not be! If they understood some of the principles set forth in this book and directed effort toward developing the detached upper register and its coordination with the rest of the voice, they would gain the tones which they secretly desire. However, in undertaking this exercise I must tell you that you may not at first be able to produce the desired tone. Your effort to achieve a virile sound on this high pitch may have produced nothing but a weak upper register tone. Even if that is the case you will have experienced a feeling of dependence upon the upper register and you will have found a sensation which is at least in part associated with the kind of high tones for which we strive. If you cannot make such a tone as that demonstrated on the recording, it is better that you make the small upper register sound than to spread your mouth, raise the tongue in the back, and sing a blatant tone. The full voiced tone which we seek will almost certainly be felt in the head, as is the small tone. The incorrect loud tone will probably be felt more in the mouth than in the head. That kind of sound must be avoided.

If an approximation of the demonstrated sound is beyond your capability at this point, the exercise should be laid aside until you have further developed the pure upper register and coordinated it through scale singing. The exercise may then be tried from time to time in the hope that you may find the means of successfully executing it.

10

Resonance and Volume

In order to discuss and to understand the matter of loudness and softness in the voice it is necessary to have some elementary knowledge of the physics of sound. Let us examine the simple characteristics of a sound wave.

Sound waves transmitted through the air are *longitudinal.* They are passed on by air molecules striking other molecules which in turn strike other molecules. These molecules striking against their neighbors create crowded areas ahead of them (*condensation*) and somewhat empty areas behind them (*rarefaction*). This phenomenon of condensation and rarefaction takes the form of waves which travel in all directions from the source of vibration to an ear which translates it into sound. This unseen action can better be understood by recalling the action of water waves, for the same phenomenon can also be transmitted by materials more solid than the rarified gas which we call air. A wave moves toward the shore *longitudinally* but it also has a *transverse* aspect. This *transverse* characteristic can be seen in the up and down motion of the wave which has a crest and a trough. The wave length is measured from the commencement of the wave's rise to the beginning of the next rise. The wave length in sound begins with the one period of condensation and ends with the beginning of the next period of condensation. In the wave of water the vertical distance from the top of the crest to the normal level of the water is the *amplitude*. The sound wave also has this same characteristic. Lower tones have longer wave lengths than higher tones. Louder tones have a greater wave *amplitude* than softer tones.

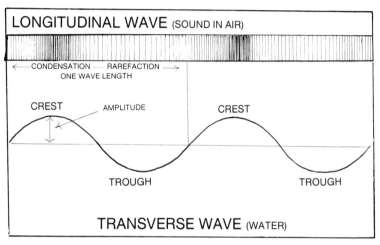

Figure 2. Diagrams illustrating transverse waves (water waves and light waves) and longitudinal waves (sound waves in the air).

The term *dynamics,* in reference to singing, is used to denote variations in the volume of the tone. This is also referred to as vocal *intensity,* or simply *loudness* or *softness. Loudness* more specifically designates the strength of the tone as heard, and vocal *intensity* denotes the strength of the tone as it is measured objectively. *Carrying power* is often an implied factor in vocal dynamics, since singing is frequently heard from a distance. All of these terms have a somewhat different connotation when they are applied to sciences other than music.

Intensity of sound is caused by two factors: first, the *amplitude* of the vibration, and second, the *surface area* set in motion by the vibrating body. Vocal sounds are caused by pulsations of breath forced through a closed glottis (the opening between the vocal cords) and are transmitted by the air molecules which the pulsations have set in motion. The force with which the air breaks through the tightly closed cords affects the loudness or softness of the tone since it is that force which sets the air into vibration and determines the *amplitude* or width of the sound wave.

Vocal tone, as it comes to our ears is affected by resonance within the body of the vocalist, by the reflection or absorption of sound on the outside, and by external objects set into sympathetic vibration by the initial sound.

There is also a relationship between the pitch of a tone and its volume. *Intensity* is proportional to the product of the *amplitude* squared and the *frequency* squared. Physicists express this with the formula ($I = a^2 f^2$). As explained earlier, *amplitude* is the width of the sound wave. *Frequency* refers to the number of vibrations per second. If the *amplitude* remains constant (i.e., if the singer uses his voice in such manner that the same pressure is used in producing tone throughout his vocal range) the higher tones will be louder because the high tones have a greater frequency of vibration than the low tones.

Intensity in the human voice is affected by three factors: (1) the force of the expelled breath (which is a coordinated action involving the muscles which expel the breath and those that close and tense the vocal cords); (2) the action of the vocal cords (that is, the amount of vocal tissue employed in

145

making the sound and the thinning or thickening of the edges of the vocal folds); (3) the increase of resonance imparted to the initial sound through surfaces and cavities of the body or the dampening effect brought about by obstruction of these resonating parts.

The human voice has three parts; a motor (the breath), a vibrator (the vocal cords), and a resonator (the cavities and some hard surfaces of the body). These three factors are the property of all musical instruments. The voice differs from mechanical instruments, however, because of the adjustability of parts of the vocal mechanism. For this reason it is a complicated and highly variable instrument which is extremely difficult to analyze. Its complications are so great and so concealed that much of its action has thus far defied the efforts of physicists and laryngologists to arrive at a thoroughly proven analysis. Description of some of its actions, therefore, remains in the realm of conjecture and theory. Some discussion, part of which is theoretical, is given here concerning the three factors controlling dynamics.

The Effect of Breath upon the Volume of Tone

The intensity of human sound is controlled in great degree by the pressure of the exhaled breath upon the vocal cords. The relationship of breath pressure and vocal intensity are generally recognized but not thoroughly understood. This pressure in the production of human sound is as much determined by the action of the vocal cords as the exhalation of the breath. Let us turn to a brief discussion of *pressure* in order that we may clearly understand the relationship between breath and vocal cords in this aspect of singing.

In order to determine the pressure involved in a given situation it is necessary to consider (1) the *force applied* and (2) the *area of the surface* which must sustain the force. If a *force* is being exerted but not resisted by any other force, such as an interrupting surface, no *pressure* is built up.

The pressure brought about by closure of the vocal cords while breath is being expelled may in some respect be understood by considering the pressure of water in a garden hose. Such pressure is greater when it flows through a small nozzle than it is when the nozzle is removed. The *applied force* in this instance remains the same but the *area of the surface* is increased. The pressure of the water flowing through the partially closed hose is increased because the water is being held back by the small opening of the nozzle. It, therefore, applies force to the inner walls of the hose which are strong enough to confine that force. This leaves the water pressure no other means of release except through the small orifice of the nozzle.

In the operation of the voice the breath is expelled (*force applied*) against vocal cords (*area of surface*). The cords, better described as vocal lips, act as a valve closing the glottis (the space between the cords when they are in an open position). If efficient sound is produced, the cords are brought so tightly together that they only separate when a breath pressure too great for them to restrain has built up beneath their closure. If the vocal cords are not brought together (that is, if the glottis is open as it is for inhaling) an extremely small amount of pressure is involved in the exhalation of the breath. The pressure is so negligible that the singer has no consciousness of it, since the size of the open glottis

147

is sufficient to allow free passage of slowly exhaled breath. If the glottis is closed enough to partially restrain the breath and produce some sound, the singer commences to feel a slight pressure and, if the cords are brought tightly enough together to produce a clear and brilliant tone, the singer feels the exertion of the breath expelling muscles and is conscious of the pressure which is present during that circumstance. The cords, like a valve, have acted as the nozzle on the hose. The breath has only been able to force its way through a small opening while force is being exerted upon a larger area of surface, the completely closed cords as well as the trachea below and the inner surfaces of the lung cavity, both of which confine the pent-up force of breath as the inner walls of the hose have confined the pent-up force of the water.

This discussion regarding the nature of *pressure* and its involvement in the production of vocal sound is included in this discussion of the voice with the hope that it will clarify thinking regarding the part played by the vocal cords themselves and will lead to a clearer understanding of the various means of controlling *volume* in human sound.

If the glottis is firmly closed, a solid pressure will be felt in the sounding of either loud or soft tones. If the muscles closing the glottis and tensing the cords continue to resist the breath force below, an increase in that breath force will result in increased pressure and a louder tone. That increase in pressure may be accomplished by contraction of the breath expelling muscles.The particular tension or adjustment of the cords will determine the pitch while the firmness of the closure will only allow the breath to escape in minute but forceful puffs. Thus, a simple increase or decrease in breath force becomes a means of altering vocal *intensity* since the breath will drive past the closed cords with lesser or greater thrust. Applying this situation to the physicists formula, the *area of surface* remains constant but the force *applied* is increased or decreased with a resulting intensification or lessening of pressure. Converted into sound wave impulses, the energy reveals itself in loudness or softness. However, in the human voice, with its delicately adjustable parts, the means of controlling *intensity* is not a simple procedure. It involves more than the increase or decrease of breath force. It particularly involves the action of the vocal cords. Let us consider more thoroughly the means of control from that source.

Control of Volume by the Vocal Cords

Photographs of the vocal cords in action have proven that a large or small part of the cords may be employed in making sound. It has also been observed that sound may be produced with the edges of the cords thickened, or with the edges thinned. Although the cords are very small (2/5 to 3/5 of an inch in length in women and 3/4 to one inch in men) they have an incredible adjustability which makes it possible to press them either tightly or lightly together, to separate them, to use only part of their thickness or part of their length. All of these manipulations can affect the volume as well as the pitch of the sound.

In order that we may understand how the vocal cords must adapt themselves for the sounding of pitch in combination with controlled *intensity*, it is necessary to understand more fully the manner in which vocal sound is produced.

149

The vocal cords do not function as the strings of a stringed instrument, but as a pair of membranous lips which, drawn together to close the glottis, are forced slightly apart by the pressure of expelled breath and drawn together again by a combination of muscular tension and their own elasticity. That elasticity, and the human capability to tighten and bring them together while at the same time blowing breath against them, makes the sounding action possible. While the cords are closed the breath is pushed against them until it builds up a pressure too great for them to withstand. Part of the closure is then forced apart. This releases enough pressure to allow the cords to snap back into position. It is like a pot of porridge boiling on a stove. Gas builds up from below, a bubble appears and breaks, the porridge fills the opening and the action is repeated. In the production of vocal sound the action is repeated at great speed, cutting the air current into a series of pulses which, through their disturbance of the atmosphere, come to our ears as sound. The pitch of the sound is determined by the number of pulsations emitted per second. If the number of these pulsations is increased, the pitch becomes higher. The frequency of pulsations is affected by the degree of tension with which the pulsating area of the vocal lips is held; by the thinness or thickness of the vibrating area; by the amount of the cords being employed, or by a combination of two or more of these factors. The volume of sound is controlled by the same factors working in coordination with breath pressure and the determinants of resonance. However, the means of obtaining *pitch* is not always the means of obtaining the desired *intensity*; in which case delicate adjustments of the vibrating cords are necessitated.

Control of Volume through Resonance

The intensity of the tone may also be affected by resonance. *Resonance* is described as the intensification and enrichment of a musical tone by means of supplimentary vibration. It results from synchronous vibrations that blend with the initial pulsations issuing from a generator of sound.

The importance of resonance in adding to the volume and tonal quality produced by various musical instruments is well known. Synchronous vibrations of the body of the violin and of the air within its body give amplification and quality to the sound produced by the vibrating string. Air vibrating within the tube out of which a trumpet is shaped intensifies the sound produced by the player's vibrating lips and gives it a characteristic quality. The principle of resonance which is demonstrated in the trumpet is the principle involved in the resonance factor of any open tube type of instrument. The quality of the tone produced by any instrument of the open tube variety is dependent upon the size and shape of the resonating chamber, and upon the manner in which the generator vibrates. Instruments of the open tube variety include the clarinet, the oboe, the bassoon, the trumpet, the tuba, the trombone, and the human voice.

The voice, well used, is a much more flexible and expressive instrument than any other. The variety of sound which it is capable of producing is not only made possible by the unusual adaptability of the vibrator, previously described, but by an unusual adjustability of the resonator. The human voice is completely unique among musical instruments in that the performer may, to a great extent, control the size and the shape of the resonance chamber.

151

The principal resonators in the voice are those body cavities which contain air. These cavities are the chest, the lower throat (pharynx), the mouth, the nose and upper throat (naso-pharynx), and the sinuses. The resonance of the voice is probably also increased to some extent by the hard surfaces of the skull and the teeth. Of all of these factors the throat itself seems to be the most important determinant of resonance. Charles F. Lindsley's report of the individual differences in voice quality listed the most active resonators of the voice in the following order of importance; the pharynx, the lower jaw (mouth), the chest, the top of the head, the nasal framework, the left and right sinuses, and the frontal sinuses.[1]

The size and shape of the vocal resonators are governed by the muscles controlling the expansion of the chest, by the vocal cords acting as a valve opening of the chest, by the epiglottis, by the action of the tongue, by the opening of the lower jaw, by the shaping of the lips, and by the uvula and soft palate (velum).

The existence of chest resonance during phonation can be tested by holding a stethoscope against the chest wall. Laboratory experiments have shown that every frequency imposed upon the atmosphere surrounding a musical wind instrument is also imposed upon the air within the player's mouth, throat, and chest cavity.[2] Since the voice is compar-

---

[1] Charles Frederick Lindsley, "Psycho-physical Determinants of Individual Differences in Voice Quality," *Psychological Bulletin*, Vol. 30 (1933), p.594.

[2] John Redfield, "Certain Anomalies in Air Column Behaviour of Wind Instruments," *Journal Acoustical Society of America*, Vol. 6 (1934), p.34.

able in acoustical principle to wind instruments, it may be assumed that air *behind* the vibrator of the human instrument is also subjected to the same frequency of vibration as that which is *past* the vibrator. In other words, air within the trachea and chest will vibrate with the same frequency as the vocal cords and will, therefore, serve as a resonator to the instrument. It may be seen from this that sound travels against the stream of air that generates it, just as it travels with the stream of air.

Maximum chest resonance may be consciously employed by the singer. No complicated controls are involved in its usage; the singer has but to comfortably expand the chest to add such resonance to the tone. The gain will be more of quality than of volume although some increase in intensity may be thus effected. The larger size of the resonating chamber will reinforce the fundamental and lower partials,[3] giving fullness to the quality. In making use of this means of resonance the singer must be warned that raising the chest to an unnaturally high position will result in tension of the lower rib muscles, as well as those of the lower back and abdomen. This is undesirable since a sustained tension in these areas will hamper natural breathing and add sympathetic tension to muscles of the throat.

---

[3]The presence or absence of (or greater or lesser strength of) particular overtones (also called harmonics or upper partials) determines the quality of a sound. All musical instruments, including the voice, produce composite sounds, consisting of the main sound (fundamental) plus a number of additional pure sounds, the overtones, which are not heard distinctly because their intensity is much less than the fundamental. See Figure 3 for an illustration of the first fifteen overtones of one particular pitch.

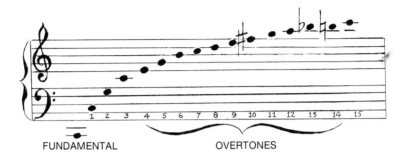

Figure 3. Diagram showing the first fifteen overtones of C^1.

The epiglottis and rear portion of the tongue enable us to adjust the size of the pharyngeal part of the resonator. The epiglottis is a thin, valve-like, cartilaginous structure that covers the glottis during swallowing, preventing the entrance of food and liquid into the larynx. It may be considered a part of the tongue since it is attached to the base portion of the tongue and is controlled in its movements by the tongue muscles. If the tongue is pulled back into the throat, as in swallowing, the epiglottis closes tightly over the opening into the larynx. If the tongue is pulled back, the epiglottis will partially block the pharynx, the most important part of the vocal resonator. When the tongue is forward, or in its most restful position, the epiglottis stands upright, leaving the throat (resonating tube) completely open. The positions may be seen in Figure 4.

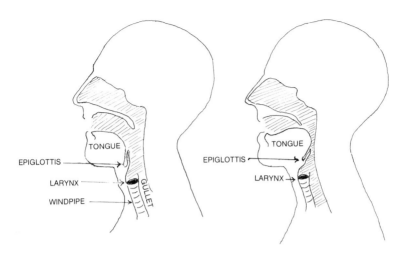

Figure 4. Illustration showing (at left) the position of the epiglottis when the tongue is in its proper position for singing and (at right) the obstructing position of tongue and epiglottis when the tongue is pulled back into the throat.

If the tongue and epiglottis are pulled backward into the throat (see Figure 5) they function as a mute, just as an object placed in the tube of a horn serves to weaken the horn sound. The free resonance of the tone will be blocked; it will be obstructed not only by the shape and position of the obstacle but also by its texture. The soft sponginess of the tongue, when placed in an obstructing position, undoubtedly acts as an absorbent of sound. The possibility of controlling dynamics and altering vocal quality through this action should be apparent. However, to use this means is to lessen the effectiveness of the voice. The dangers involved in using this to lessen volume will be described in the following chapter.

Still another means of modifying the shape and size of the resonance chamber is provided by the lower jaw and the front part of the tongue. This requires little explanation. If we move the jaw, it is possible for us to feel the alteration of the size of the mouth chamber. A glance at Figure 5 will show something of the extent to which this change may be made. It may also be seen that changing positions of the visible part of the tongue will alter the shape

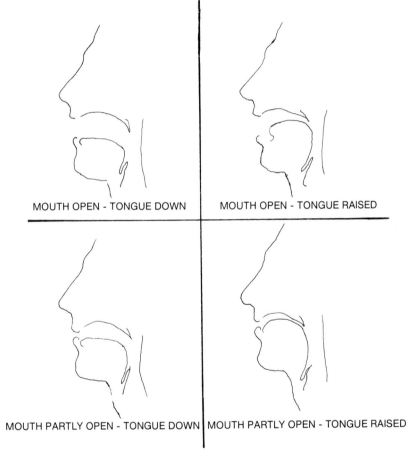

MOUTH OPEN - TONGUE DOWN | MOUTH OPEN - TONGUE RAISED

MOUTH PARTLY OPEN - TONGUE DOWN | MOUTH PARTLY OPEN - TONGUE RAISED

Figure 5. A diagram showing alterations in the size and shape of the oral resonator through jaw and tongue movement.

and size of the oral portion of the resonator. Alterations of the resonance chamber by means of the jaw and that part of the tongue lying within the mouth are the principal means of producing vowels. The adjustment of jaw position, when coupled with a low placement of the tongue, is also a natural and effective means of altering the intensity and tonal quality of the voice.

The ability to shape the lips provides us with still another means of modifying the vocal resonator. Changes in lip position alter the quality of vocal tone just as changes in the shape of the open end of a wind instrument transform its quality. The bell portion of a French horn is more widely flared than that of a trumpet. This difference in shape is a factor in the quality difference of the two instruments. The shape of the bell of any lip vibrating wind instrument affects its tonal color. If the terminal part of the tube is greatly flared, the intensity of the highest partials is reduced. The tone also comes out with greater diffusion. If the bell at the end of the tube is small, the instrument yields a brighter and more penetrating quality. Obviously the human mouth is incapable of assuming the dimensions and shape of either the French horn or the trumpet but some alterations are possible and the principle demonstrated by the varied shape of horns is applicable to the shaping of the human resonator. Changes in mouth position may add interesting tonal color to the voice and may also assist the singer in controlling subtle gradations of volume.

Volume and **quality** of tone are both affected by **resonance**. For that reason it often becomes difficult to separate volume and resonance in singing. Part of the difficulty stems from the fact that an

157

aesthetic result in singing is often accomplished by an illusion. A soft tone is sometimes not a softer tone at all, but one of different quality. However, it is not important that these aspects of singing be separated here, since both relate to the expressiveness of the voice and these remarks are only made in the hope of indicating how marvelously flexible and infinitely expressive the human voice may be. Such contemplation inevitably leads to the realization that the greatest marvel of all is that the highly complex vocal mechanism, which may operate in a variety of ways, is capable of functioning with great efficiency and expressive power, if the correct impulse is delivered from the mind. It is for this reason that discussion of the mechanics of the voice has been assigned to this late chapter.

Establishment of Natural Tone is the Basis on Which to Build Vocal Shading.

The most important part of vocal production, the establishment of the basic natural sound, must be achieved with something of the free spontaneity described in earlier chapters. If any attempts are made to control the muscular apparatus of the voice before a correct mental concept of the tone has been established, they are almost certain to end in failure. To approach the problems of the voice through conscious control of muscles is to work backward in the design of nature. The mind is the superintendent in this operation. Attention may be given to one or two details in the singing process, but we cannot consciously control all of the complicated coordinations which are involved in the processes of beautiful vocal expression. When the voice is produced in the manner that nature intended, it is far more responsive in conveying expression. The mind dictates that which is to be expressed and the natural voice delivers the expression. The voice becomes a reflection of the mind.

There is still another aspect of resonance that should be considered. The previous discussion has only been concerned with the resonator within the human body and the effect of this resonator upon the vocal tone. Resonance affecting the intensity of sound and its quality may also be provided by the surroundings in which a singer or speaker performs. Reverberation from the hard surfaces of an auditorium increases the loudness of the sound and enriches its quality. If the initial sound has that purity which gives it carrying power, its sound waves will reach more surfaces and will consequently be augmented and enriched to a greater degree than the tone which lacks carrying power. From this it may be seen that an unclear tone which is loud in a small room may lack power in a large auditorium. Such a tone lacks power in the larger surroundings because the initial sound, deficient in carrying power, dissipates its strength before it reaches the listener's ear or the reflecting surfaces of the auditorium. If the tone is diffused and weak when it reaches the reflecting surfaces, it deprives itself of that resonance which is gained through reverberation. Consequently, vocal passages may be reduced in volume by the elimination of carrying power. However, if this means of reducing power is used, the tones will lack that vitality and shimmering beauty which characterize the best of vocal utterance. It will also have been acquired by a muffling of the tone with the throat in a partially closed position. This hampers the best vocal usage.

The singer gains the muted effect by a retraction of the tongue. The deleterious effect of this tongue position upon freely emitted tone will be discussed later.

However, a further skill in the use of the voice can be consciously cultivated after the basic natural tone is firmly established. It is for that reason that this chapter has been devoted to a more involved discussion of vocal mechanics. If the student proceeds with the exercises outlined in the earlier chapters and is successful in establishing a free tonal production, he will have in his possession the kind of natural voice which many great singers have brought to a teacher for refinement. The student, with no consciousness of having done so, will have brought about a correct usage of the vocal cords and a correct functioning of the vocal resonator. In doing so, he will have developed some awareness of muscular and vibratory sensations. If he has done it long enough, he certainly will have gained some consciousness of his manner of opening the throat. He will recognize, by comparison with his freely emitted sound, the tone which is not free; he will recognize one which is muffled. These are invaluable guides to his future course as a singer. He must take care that he does not lose them in his quest for additional vocal effects.

The preliminary exercises in this book have already given the means of cultivating the maximum strength of the voice. That strength has revealed itself because the efforts to produce sound in a spontaneous, natural manner have brought about a marvelous muscular coordination; the larynx has been held firmly in position, the vocal cords have come closely and tightly together, a large portion of the cords have resisted the force of the air seeking to be expelled, the tongue and epiglottis have been in a forward position, and other parts of the resonator have been adjusted to create maximum sound without strain. Nothing more need be said about the loud tone except to warn the singer that it must be produced in this manner and must not be forced beyond the limits of comfortable singing.

It is with the soft tone and the many shadings that lie between soft and loud that we are now to be concerned. Excepting that softness gained through the register control which is to be discussed later, attention must *not* be given to the soft tone until the natural freedom has been achieved. When the free tone is thoroughly established, the singer will understand his manner of opening the throat and will be able to retain the openness when singing softly. He will also be able to recapture all possible resonance and power, even after continued pianissimo singing.

The soft tone, or the tone which is any degree less than loud, may be produced in different ways in different parts of the voice. In any range of the voice it can be accomplished by pulling the tongue back into the throat and thereby deadening the resonance. This is the least desirable means, however, and once again the singer should be reminded that it must be avoided. When the tongue is retracted, the correct functioning of the hyoid bone and the extrinsic muscles of the larynx become an impossibility, thereby disturbing the natural and most effective coordinations of the voice. An obstructing position of the tongue decreases the volume of tone by the elimination of its maximum resonance, but it substitutes a restricted sound for a free one, it replaces a clear sound with a dull one, and it takes away much of the vibrant beauty which can come to the voice when it is properly used. To some small degree it will probably be unconsciously used as our means of expression but it should not be sought. It is imperative that the singer should always strive for the most complete opening of the throat. If he does so he will be losing one means of softening a tone but, at the same time, he will be taking steps to gain a far more effective means of singing softly. He will then rely upon the cooperative actions of the breath and vocal cords to obtain his control of dynamics.

Enumerating once more the means of decreasing volume: it may be accomplished (1) by a reduction in the force of air which is brought against the vocal cords, (2) by vocal cord adjustments, (3) by reduction in the size of the resonator, or (4) by a combination of two or more of these means. The vocalist will quickly recognize when he is applying a lesser force of air to the vibrator and will have no difficulty in doing so. However, delicate adjustments in the pressure are necessary for vocal control. These adjustments involve a fine coordination between the muscles expelling the breath and the muscles controlling the tension of the cords. This coordination, like that involved in most human skills, is brought about by continued practice intelligently directed toward the accomplishment of the desired objective. Many simple exercises or passages from songs could be used; passages which require soft singing, or a diminishing of tone.

Since it is undesirable that the tongue should block the resonating chambers, the principal reduction in the size of the resonator must be made by the lower jaw and lips which alter the size and shape of the mouth cavity. As the tone is reduced in volume the mouth and jaw may be slowly closed until only a small opening remains. This closing of the jaw may bring about a slight alteration of the vowel but will enhance the beauty of the pianissimo.

A reduction in the size of the chest cavity will accomplish little in achieving a soft tone. An expanded position of the chest adds little to vocal power and that which it adds to quality should not be sacrificed.

The tone can also be reduced in intensity by only partially closing the glottis. If the vocal cords are not brought firmly together, the breath pressure is reduced and the tone is softened through loss of energy. A concomitant breathiness of sound will result. This manner of lessening the intensity utilizes a principle of inefficiency; breath is lost in the operation. It will certainly be used occasionally by the sensitive dramatic artist but it should not be persistently used; needed breath and beauty of tone are lost by its employment.

Controlling Loudness and Softness through the Coordination of Registers.

Control of the muscles involved in the coordination of registers plays a great part in controlling intensity. The production of the very lowest tones of the voice is assigned to the low register, and the highest tones are properly transferred to the high register. In between, where the registers overlap, the dynamics of the voice may be controlled in part by a working together of the two registers. When the low register is used in the upper part of its range it can only be loud. When the high register is used in the

163

low part of its range it can only be soft. The muscles involved in producing the upper register should take over an increasing amount of the effort as the singer ascends the scale in normal singing. However, the normal volume of tone in the upper middle part of the voice may be increased by involving the low register muscles to a greater extent than usual. Likewise, throughout the middle range the sound may be softened by drawing more than the normal amount of high register into the tone.

This may be better understood by studying Figure 6. The diagram illustrates my belief that in well produced voices the low register muscles carry less of the burden as the voice ascends in pitch. Above and below the coordinated area the upper and lower registers are separately employed. The pitches indicated in the diagram can only be taken as an approximation of the pitches at which adjustments are made. The overlapping registers may be coordinated within a slightly different range with different individuals.

In Figure 6 it will be seen that a tenor singing with medium intensity the E written for him on the fourth treble space, but sounded one octave lower, is employing an equal proportion of low and high registers. If he wishes to increase the volume of this E, he can do so by drawing more of the low register into the tone and at this pitch he might very well do it without placing undue strain upon the voice. He might employ this same means in reinforcing tones several notes higher but if he forces a great amount of low register into the very highest notes within this coordinated range, he will certainly bring about a vocal strain. The strain will probably be apparent in the sound. The singer might employ

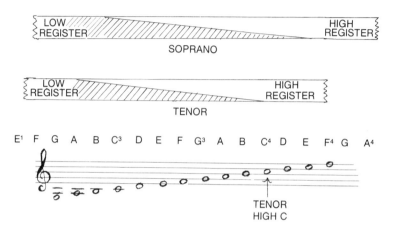

Figure 6. A diagram showing the area in which low and high registers coordinate in soprano and tenor voices. Do not forget that music for tenor written in the treble clef is actually sung one octave lower. The coordinated area in alto voices is only slightly lower in pitch than that area in the soprano voice. Coordination between registers in bass voices lies a few tones lower than in tenor voices.

it occasionally without harmful effects but great power persistently achieved by pushing the low register into the highest tones of this range will certainly result in a premature deterioration of the voice. Conversely, if the tenor wishes to sing the E more softly, he may do so by employing more than the normal amount of high register. He may also do this for pitches above or below the E and this may be done without danger of straining the voice. However, if the high register is presistently and exclusively used for the lowest notes of its range, a vocally harmful breathiness will result. The part played by the registers in controlling intensity is even better exemplified by considering the diminishing of volume on a single tone within this coordinated part of the range. If the tenor wishes to diminish the E, or any other tone so coordinated, he will do so by gradually decreasing the amount of low register employed in the production of this note. If a complete *diminuendo* is executed, he will gradually withdraw all low register from the tone, sustaining the final duration of sound with the upper register alone. A *crescendo* from very soft to very loud, in opposite manner, will be largely accomplished by adding low register to the tone. A soft high tone will probably be produced by the high register alone.

Reference has been made to the employment of more or less of a particular register because it seems more easily understood by the singer. Of course, we are actually referring to a greater or lesser degree of employment of those muscles principally involved in the production of tones in that register.

All voices may utilize this means of controlling volume. One voice classification, the tenor, has been referred to in order that reference might be made to a specific pitch and range. However, the same expressive usage of registers is employed by sopranos, altos, baritones, and basses, if the voices are properly produced. The overlapping of registers and the coordinated range of basses and baritones are only slightly lower than those of the tenor voice. The overlapping of registers in the female voice takes place on approximately the same pitches as that in the male voice. However, it must be remembered that the female voice is approximately one octave higher than the male voice.

That part of the scale in which coordination between registers of the male voice takes place may be considered the middle of the range, if the fully developed high register is taken into consideration (see Figure 1, Chapter 5). However, since the male singer is not called upon to use the complete upper register, the span of coordinated registration must be thought of as lying in the upper middle and high parts of his voice.

Women, on the other hand, are required to use much of their high registers and so, in practical singing, the coordination between registers takes place in the lower middle and middle range of their voices. This part of the voice must, therefore, be thought of as that in which volume may be controlled through the coordinated use of the registers (see Figure 6).

Some knowledge of the mechanical means of controlling dynamics in the voice should be of help to the singer in developing a command of this aspect of singing and in calculating desired vocal effects. However, if a sensitive singer who produces his voice well strives to convey the intended expressions of song, he will in the course of time acquire skill in handling dynamic shadings. Coordinations which control this means of expression will be developed naturally by the impulses emanating from imagination, remembrance of sounds, and the natural human instinct for expressiveness. Nevertheless, conscious coordinations may be cultivated and a skill in controlling vocal dynamics may be acquired through practice. It will not be acquired without effort. It will take time and perseverance.

References have been made to such maneuvers as the thinning and thickening of the edges of the vocal cords, and to their stretching. In the singer's effort to accomplish different effects it is not for a moment thought that conscious effort will be made to manipulate the cords. It is certain that muscular control is involved in the delicate adjustments, but there is still some scientific uncertainty regarding the specific involvement of the muscles.

It is not necessary for the singer to know exactly what is happening; such knowledge would be of little use. Nevertheless, a general knowledge that such action is possible should inspire the singer to persevere in his efforts to achieve the desired results.

Exercises for the development of skill in coordinating the two registers of the voice have been given in Chapter Ten. The importance of those exercises cannot be overemphasized. They should be practiced daily for years. Indeed, the singer should never cease to practice them. If a fine coordination between registers is developed, the entire voice is enhanced.

In addition to those exercises given in Chapter Ten, the following exercises will also be useful. Singing scales or sustained tones, however, will do nothing for the singer unless he is using the voice correctly when he practices. They will only be helpful if the singer uses them as assignments to be executed with freely produced tones.

Exercise for Developing Control of Loudness and Softness (for Men or Women)

The pitches shown here are not mandatory. The singer should select notes from the high to the low part of his singing range and apply the technique. In addition to the crescendos and diminuendoes indicated, the singer should also strive to sing tones that are very soft, avoiding the muffled effects which have been discussed.

11

The Tongue and the Hyoid Bone

Look into the mouth of any crying baby and you will observe that the tongue is cupped and depressed into a deep groove on the floor of the mouth (see Figure 7). The posterior portion is drawn downward and forward, leaving the throat passage to the larynx open to its fullest extent. That part of the tongue lying within the baby's mouth is trough-like in shape, the center line of the visible tongue from its anterior to its posterior portion being in its lowest possible position. The tongue's trough-like appearance is accentuated by what appears to be a slightly raised position of the sides and tip. If an identical position of the tongue is assumed by an adult, the sides and tip do not appear to be raised because the teeth conceal the underside.

This tongue position is invariably associated with the vocal production of children during the first few years of their lives. Thereafter, it appears but infrequently; seldom in cultivated sounds, more often in spontaneous laughter or the terrified screaming of women. In our quest for the natural manner of producing sound this tongue position is significant. What can give us a more direct clue to the natural manner of using the voice than observation of the tiny infant, or the adult who, through the force of extreme emotion, reverts to natural instinct?

The ability to produce clear, far carrying sound is as consistent with the new born baby as the groove which appears in its tongue when it makes such a sound. Why does the human being so often lose that clarity of sound when he passes from babyhood?

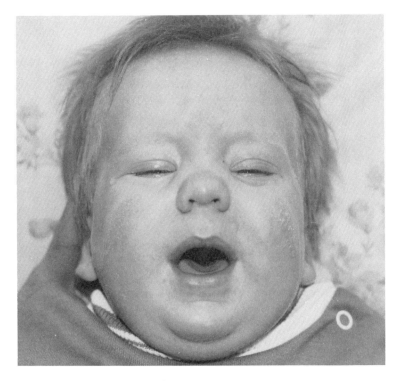

Figure 7. Photograph of crying baby.

The detrimental effects wrought upon the voice by mental impressions, inhibitions, and mistaken ideas have previously been discussed. Man's spoken language may also contribute to poor vocal production. The vocal impairment through speech may in some instances be attributable to incorrect muscular habits which, through a kind of laziness in the formation of vowels and consonants, have become a part of tonal production. Language, with its great variety of sounds,[1] is a thing devised by man. It is far more complex than anything intended by nature or anything used by animals or babies. The sounds from which language is formed are made in a variety of ways; the tongue playing the greatest part in the formation of all vowels and most consonants. The rapid changes of tongue position which the human being is required to make when speaking often lead him to a loss of that position of the tongue which is basically right for the formation of sound.

The correct position of the tongue is not only demonstrated by the crying baby, it is demonstrated by the best singers in the world (e.g., see Figure 8). Again and again it may be seen in the mouths of great singers as they hurl out their ringing, resonant tones. With some, the grooved aspect is as perfect in formation as that of the baby. With others it is present, but less perfectly formed. Some operatic tenors, basses, or baritones exaggerate the cupped position to such an extent that the tip of the tongue turns upward, disclosing the underside. I do not believe that such a position should be cultivated since it restricts flexibility in the tip of the tongue. However, it bears such similarity to the tongue position of the crying child that it must be considered an indication of natural action. With some the front part of the tongue is slightly

---

[1]Approximately fifty vowel and consonant sounds are used in the English language.

arched but the back part is down and in such position as to indicate that the posterior portion, out of sight in the throat, is pressed forward.[2]

Figure 8. A grooved position of the tongue is clearly visible in this photograph of soprano Leonie Rysanek in an actual performance of the title role of the opera Salome by Richard Strauss.

The lowered tongue position is generally only revealed when the singer is producing one of the "open" vowels. On such sounds the mouth is opened sufficiently to enable a viewer to see the tongue. During the sounding of the other vowels (EE, IH, OO, Ü) the mouth is closed to such an extent that observation is difficult. However, close examination

---

[2]The grooved tongue is almost never to be seen in the mouths of people who sing badly. Their tongues are often raised and retracted if their voices are dull and lacking in carrying power. When the tongue is flaired and raised in the back the tone is usually blatant.

174

has convinced me that the best of singers also produce a clear, ringing OO with the tongue in the low, grooved position. X-ray photographs have shown that even on these vowels the posterior portion is drawn forward and the epiglottis is in its erect position.[3] Although it is exceptional, even among the best of singers, I have many times seen an EE (which requires a raising of the tongue) produced with a well defined groove.

In most instances the singer has little awareness of the tongue position. The voice, with the exceptionally fine singer, functions naturally and the tongue position is an indication that the voice is being produced in that natural manner. The great singer has often produced his voice in this fashion for many years, perhaps for his entire lifetime, and, consequently, gives little attention to a muscular action which would be noteworthy to one who had never experienced it. There are great singers, however, who have associated the low grooved position with the correctly produced tone. Some have, over a period of years, become aware of the position and others have consciously cultivated it. Some have found amusement in performing "tricks" with the tongue and in so doing have discovered the grooved position and associated it with the best of their singing.

Caruso's biographer and associate, Salvatore Fucito, recalled that the great tenor in childish fun

---

[3]G. Oscar Russell, *Speech and Voice* (The Macmillan Co. 1931), Figures 96 and 97 p.134, Figure 101 p.136, Figure 156 p.162.

Dr. Raoul Husson, "Special Physiology in Singing with Power," *The Bulletin*, XIV (October 1957), p.14-15.

sometimes amused his friends by thrusting his tongue out and shaping it into a deeply cupped position. It is conceivable that Caruso's ability to perform this trick was in some way related to his masterful ability to use his voice. The trick may have come about through observation of his tongue action while singing, or it may have developed entirely from an interest in a childish prank. If the latter was the case, it is possible that the skill better enabled him to control the tongue muscles while singing.

The muffling effect attributable to a pulled back tongue and epiglottis has already been discussed. It is only necessary to have an elementary knowledge of acoustics to understand how the free emission of sound can be blocked in the throat by an obstructing position of these two organs. With this respect it is easy to understand the desirability of pressing the unseen posterior portion of the tongue against the front wall of the throat.

There is still another reason why the contracted, deeply grooved position of the tongue is desirable in singing but an attempt to explain this requires some description of the intricate muscular mechanism of the throat. No description of this system can be made very simple, but since it seems imperative that the serious student of voice should have some understanding of one of the most significant actions of the vocal apparatus, such a description is offered here. If the reader does not have knowledge of the muscles of the throat and tongue, he will find that even a meager description can only be absorbed slowly. If he will take time to absorb such an explanation, however, it should give him a general understanding of how the action of specific muscles may affect the vocal production.

When the child cries or the masterful vocalist sings, the tongue has been pulled into a grooved position by a contraction of the *hyo-glossus* muscle. This muscle is attached from the underside of the tongue to the *hyoid* bone, which is a horseshoe shaped bone situated in the throat just above the *larynx*. Contraction of the *hyo-glossus* muscle brings about a tilting action of this bone, as well as a grooving of the tongue. It is probable that this action of the *hyoid* bone has much to do with the production of firm, resonant tones; particularly in the upper range of the voice. To understand how this may be, let us look further.

In the production of sound, the vocal cords may be brought into a desired state of tension by tiny muscles within the voice box. These muscles, located entirely within the larynx, are termed *intrinsic* muscles. The cords may also be tensed by muscles which are attached to points outside the larynx, either connecting the two principal cartilages of the larynx, or connecting one to an adjacent part of the body. Muscles attached directly or indirectly to the outside of the larynx are called *extrinsic* laryngeal muscles. Certain of these muscles directly control the movements of the larynx, others determine such movements through their control of the *hyoid* bone. Movements of the larynx, brought about by the action of *extrinsic* muscles, may stretch the vocal cords to greater length and tension during the production of tone, thereby making it possible to employ a greater body of the vocal folds in their breath resisting function. The action of these muscles is therefore of great importance to the singer who, for the production of resonant and powerful tones, must bring a large part of the vocal cords into play, and who, for the production of ringing tones in the high range of the voice, must employ unusual strength in the cord stretching action.

Two cartilages (the *thyroid* and the *cricoid*), one bone (the *hyoid*), and the tongue (*glossus*) are of particular interest to us in understanding the effect which the *extrinsic* muscles may have upon the stretching of the vocal cords.

The two cartilages, bound closely together by muscles and ligaments, form the larynx which in men is commonly called "the Adam's apple." An understanding of their shape may be gained from examination of Figures 9 and 10. The *cricoid* cartilage is the uppermost segment of the windpipe

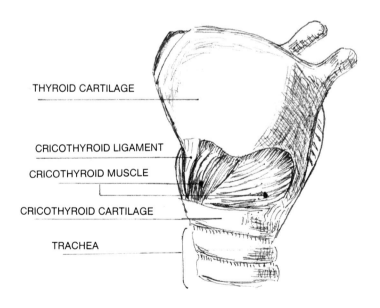

THYROID CARTILAGE

CRICOTHYROID LIGAMENT

CRICOTHYROID MUSCLE

CRICOTHYROID CARTILAGE

TRACHEA

Figure 9. Exterior of the larynx as seen from the side.

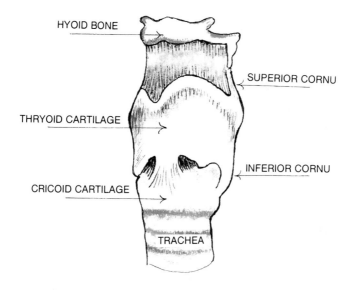

HYOID BONE

SUPERIOR CORNU

THRYOID CARTILAGE

INFERIOR CORNU

CRICOID CARTILAGE

TRACHEA

Figure 10. The larynx and hyoid bone from the front.

(*trachea*). It is a complete ring, the front of which is similar in size to the other segments of the *trachea*. The back part of this ring, however, differs considerably from the other segments of the windpipe; it is approximately three times as wide as the front of the ring. The *thyroid* cartilage is mounted above the *cricoid*, its lower horns extending down over the sides of the posterior portion of the *cricoid*, and its upper horns furnishing a point of connection with the *hyoid* bone above it (see Fig. 10). The shield-like shape of the thyroid cartilage resembles a V with the point of the V placed at the front.

The vocal cords are horizontally situated above the windpipe, attached in front to the *thyroid* cartilage and in the rear to the tiny *arytaenoid* cartilages which are, in turn, attached to the *cricoid* (see Figures 11, 12, and 13).

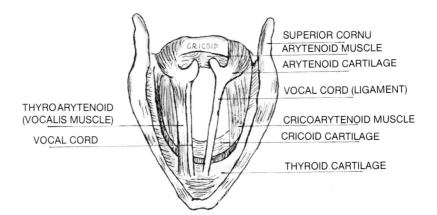

Figure 11. The larynx as seen from above. The illustration eliminates some muscles and membranes in order to disclose the relative positions of the *thyroid, cricoid,* and *arytenoid* cartilages, as well as the *vocalis, arytenoid,* and *cricoarytenoid* muscles.

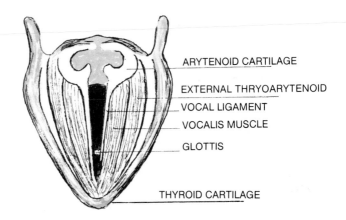

Figure 12. The larynx as seen from above. Muscles stripped from Fig. 11 are replaced in this illustration so that the valve-like character of the larynx may be seen. The vocal ligaments with their attached muscles are displayed in an open position, as for breathing. The valve opening (*glottis*) may be closed for phonation by a rotation of the *arytenoid* cartilages.

180

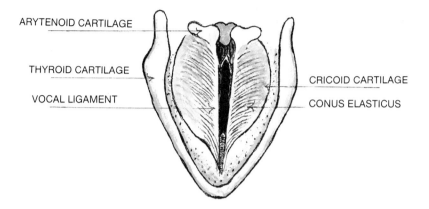

ARYTENOID CARTILAGE

THYROID CARTILAGE

VOCAL LIGAMENT

CRICOID CARTILAGE

CONUS ELASTICUS

Figure 13. The *conus elasticus*, framework for the muscular structure of the vocal folds. This tough curtain-like membrane is attached to the vocal ligament as well as to the major cartilages of the larynx; the upper surface of the *cricoid*, the lower surface of the *thyroid*, and the lower surface of the *arytenoids*.

The *thyroid* cartilage, although joined to the *cricoid* by muscles and ligaments, is somewhat free to glide forward away from the *cricoid*, or to be raised in the posterior portion. If either of these movements takes place, the cords are lengthened and stretched. It is the action of *extrinsic* muscles of the larynx and muscles attached to the *hyoid* bone that bring about such movements. In so doing they play a highly important role in the larger stretching actions of the vocal cords.

The following tables list those *extrinsic* muscles of the larynx which are involved in its raising or lowering. Those which raise the larynx are called the *suprahyoideus* muscles. Those that lower the larynx are called the *infrahyoideus*. Such muscles are usually designated in the singular although they exist in pairs. They are named for their points of attachment.

TABLE 1. A list of the five *suprahyoideus* muscles which serve to lift the larynx.

Digastricus

Points of attachment	Lower jaw to *mastoid* process of the skull.
Function	Pulls *hyoid* bone upward and backward.

Stylohyoideus

Points of attachment	*Styloid* process of the skull near the inner ear to the *hyoid* bone.
Function	Raises *hyoid* bone and larynx.

Mylohyoideus

Points of attachment	Lower jaw to *hyoid* bone.
Function	Raises *hyoid* bone and larynx. Supplies a muscular floor for the mouth cavity.

Geniohyoideus

Points of attachment	Forepart of jaw to *hyoid* bone.
Function	Raises *hyoid* bone and larynx.

Genioglossus

Points of attachment	Front of lower jaw to tongue and *hyoid* bone.
Function	Lifts *hyoid* bone and larynx. Draws tongue down to *hyoid* bone when *hyoid* bone is made firm by the muscles which pull the *hyoid* bone downward.

TABLE 2. A list of the four *infrahyoideus* muscles which serve to lower the *hyoid* bone and larynx.

Sternohyoideus

Points of attachment	Lower end of the *clavicle* and *sternum* to the *hyoid* bone.
Function	Lowers the *hyoid* bone and the larynx.

Sternothyroideus

Points of attachment	*Sternum* to *thyroid* cartilage.
Function	Draws larynx or *thryoid* cartilage downward. It may also assist the *cricothyroideus* in tilting the *thyroid* cartilage downward and drawing it forward.

Thyrohyoideus

Points of attachment	Sides of *thyroid* cartilage to lower border of the greater cornu of the *hyoid* bone.
Function	Pulls *hyoid* bone downward and depresses larynx. This muscle may lift the larynx when the *hyoid* bone ascends since the two are attached.

Omohyoideus

Points of attachment	*Clavicle* (farther back than the *sternohyoideus*) to the *hyoid* bone.
Function	Depresses larynx and *hyoid* bone. It may also carry the larynx backward and to one or the other side.

It is a marvelous mechanism. These muscles functioning in the routine and emergency demands of living probably never perform singly but in co-ordination with others, very much of the time in opposition. That is, the desired action may be brought about by certain muscles pulling down-ward while other muscles pull upward. Certainly most of it happens without conscious control. When one considers that the production of sound is de-pendent upon these muscles, as well as the nine sets of muscles which control the *hyoid* bone (to be described), the delicate maneuvering of those muscles within the larynx, and those which bring about the expulsion of breath, it seems completely incredible!

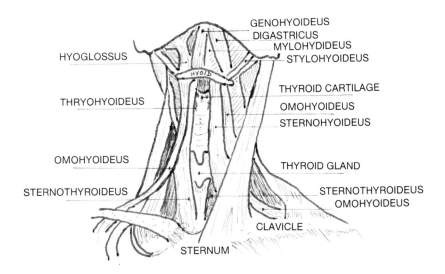

Figure 14. The controlling musculature of the *hyoid* bone (front view).

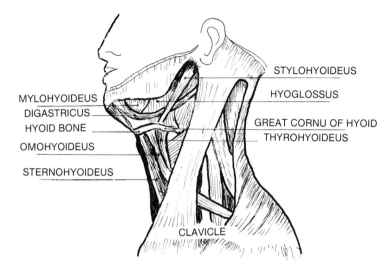

STYLOHYOIDEUS
HYOGLOSSUS
GREAT CORNU OF HYOID
THYROHYOIDEUS

MYLOHYOIDEUS
DIGASTRICUS
HYOID BONE
OMOHYOIDEUS

STERNOHYOIDEUS

CLAVICLE

Figure 15. The controlling musculature of the *hyoid* bone (side view).

Two other muscles, unattached to the *hyoid* bone, may also have an elevating effect upon the larynx. Their function must be considered in understanding the part played by the *hyoid* bone in lengthening and stretching the vocal cords. These muscles are the *stylopharyngeus* and the *palatopharyngeus*.

The *stylopharyngei* arise at the base of the styloid processes, bone projections inside the skull near the ear. They join with the *palatopharyngei* and are inserted into the posterior border of the thyroid cartilage.

The *palatopharyngei* are supported at one end by the interlaced membranes and muscles of the soft palate. Part of the other end of these muscles terminates in the central portion of the pharynx, and part of it is attached to the posterior border of the *thyroid* cartilage.

A contraction of these muscles will raise only the back of the *thyroid* cartilage if the front part of the cartilage is held down. The tilting action of the larynx is one that is of great interest to singers since it almost certainly plays an important part in stretching the vocal cords for the production of voluminous tones, particularly in the upper part of the range.

The keystone to the tilting action of the *thyroid* cartilage is the positioning of the *hyoid* bone. If it is held firmly in a downward tilted position when the *thyroid* cartilage is pulled upward by the *palato-pharyngei* muscles, it arrests the upward movement of the front part of the *thyroid* but allows the back portion to rise and bring about the tilting action previously mentioned. The importance of the *hyoid* bone must not be minimized in this leverage action. If something does not counteract the upward pulling of the *stylopharyngei* and *palatopharyngei* muscles, the larynx and *hyoid* will rise. This unnatural raising of the larynx, so detrimental to the natural functioning of the voice, is frequently to be observed in human efforts to sing. The scrawny neck of an aspiring young singer may expose the Adam's apple sufficiently to enable one to see it slide high up under the chin as he mades a desperate but unsuccessful attempt to negotiate a high tone. If the larynx is pulled far out of its natural position, either *above* or *below*, we cannot expect that it will be able to perform its natural function in making sound; no other part of the body functions well when it is out of its natural position and state of balance.

We are scarcely aware of the action of the *extrinsic* muscles of the larynx. For the most part, their action is not visible to us and we have paid little attention to their behaviour. The muscles are continually performing many functions but we have little conscious control over their movements. Some of the muscles which govern the action of the *hyoid* bone are an exception, they may be brought more directly under our conscious control. These muscles have attachment to the tongue and, since the tongue is at least partially visible, and, since its position in the mouth makes it more easily felt than some throat muscles, we are able to gain a greater awareness of their movements.

Here is a description of the *hyoid* bone and the muscular system which controls it. The *hyoid* bone, which is not attached to any immediately adjacent bone, is shaped like the letter U (see Figure 16). It is situated in a horizontal position between the larynx and lower jaw with the horns, which give it the U shape, extending straight back, surrounding the pharynx.

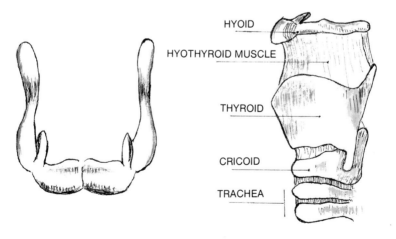

Figure 16. The *hyoid* bone, as viewed from above (at left) and its position above the *thryoid* cartilage (at right).

An intricate muscular system which attaches itself to the *hyoid* bone from several other parts of the body makes it possible to move the bone in various directions. The nine sets of muscles which control the possible movements of the *hyoid* bone are outlined below and illustrated in Figure 17.

TABLE 3. A list of the muscles which control the *hyoid* bone.

Thyrohyoideus

Points of attachment	*Thyroid* cartilage to *hyoid.*
Function	Serves to draw the *thyroid* cartilage and the *hyoid* bone closer together.

Omohyoideus

Points of attachment	*Clavicle* to *hyoid* bone.
Function	Lowers the *hyoid* bone.

Sternohyoideus

Points of attachment	*Sternum* to *hyoid.*
Function	*Lowers the hyoid* bone.

Mylohyoideus

Points of attachment	Lower jaw to *hyoid.*
Function	*Draws hyoid* forward and raises it.

Geniohyoideus

Points of attachment	Chin to *hyoid.*
Function	Draws *hyoid* forward and upward.

Stylohyoideus
Points of attachment   *Styloid* process to *hyoid.*

Function   Pulls *hyoid* upward and back-
                            ward. Anchors *hyoid* to skull.

Digastric
Points of attachment   *Mastoid* process to *hyoid.*

Function   Raises *hyoid* and pulls it back-
                            ward. Anchors *hyoid* to skull.

Hyoglossus and
Chondroglossus
Points of attachment   Tongue to *hyoid*

Function   *Controls the relationship*
                            between tongue and hyoid.
                            Makes possible the lifting of the
                            back part of the *hyoid* with its
                            consequent lowering of the front
                            part of the *hyoid* bone.

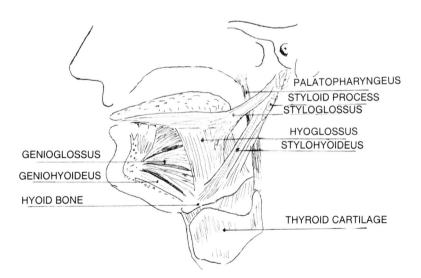

Figure 17. Muscles controlling the action of the *hyoid* bone.

189

The *hyoglossus* and *chondroglossus* are actually one muscle. *Hyoglossus* is the name applied by some anatomists to the anterior portion of the muscle and *chondroglossus* is used to describe the posterior portion. Future references in this discussion will refer to the entire muscle as the *hyoglossus.*

At the present time very little can be stated with authority concerning the exact behaviour of the *extrinsic* laryngeal muscles and their part in the production of vocal tone. Very few extensive studies of their complicated action have been made and many obstacles stand in the way of accurate and complete analysis of that action.[4] Therefore, the reader must be reminded that most statements concerning the effect of specific muscular contraction upon the vocal production are in the realm of conjecture.

However, one thing can be stated with authority — the *extrinsic* muscles of the larynx perform an important function in the larger movements of the vocal cords. This is brought about by these muscles as they slide or tilt the *thyroid cartilage upon the*

---

[4]L.E. Kenyon, "Significance of the extrinsic musculature of the larynx," *J.A.M.A.*, vol. 79 p.428.

R. Sokolowsky, "Effect of the extrinsic laryngeal muscles on voice production," *Arch. Otolar.*, 38 (1943).

Dr. Aatto A. Sonninen, "The Role of the External Laryngeal Muscles in Length-adjustment of the Vocal Cords in Singing," *Supplementum 130, Acta-Otolaryngologica* 3, (Stockholm 1956). An article concerning this report by William Vennard was published in *The Bulletin*, official magazine of the National Association of Teachers of Singing, on May 15, 1959. Mr. Vennard refers to page 74 of the Sonninen report as reference for the statement given above.

cricoid, its adjoining part. Such movement elongates and tenses the vocal cords in such manner that a larger mass of the cords is brought into action during phonation. This larger mass provides a greater area of resistance, but not necessarily a greater area of vibration.

Some evidence indicates that, when the head is in normal position, contraction of the *sternothyroid* muscle draws the *thyroid* and *cricoid* cartilages of the larynx closer together and consequently brings about some stretching of the vocal cords.[5] A similar action and result can also be achieved by contraction of the *cricothyroid* muscle which connects the two cartilages of the larynx (see Figure 9). It is not clear whether or not the action of these muscles affects the vocal cords in producing tone throughout an extended range of pitch but it is suspected that it plays its most important part in assisting with the production of low tones. The upward pulling muscles working in coordination with those which control the movements of the *hyoid* bone probably exert a more important effect upon the production of resonant high tones.

Here is an explanation of how such a coordinated action is probably used by great singers in the production of voluminous high tones. When the impulse to sing is communicated, by way of nerve channels, to the muscles of the vocal mechanism, many coordinate their actions to bring about the desired sound. Muscles used for the forceful exhalation of breath spring into action. *Intrinsic* muscles of the larynx close the *glottis* and assist in bringing the cords into the proper state of tension for the

[5]Ibid, Sonninen.

191

creation of the intended sound. Muscles of the jaw and mouth shape those parts to form the sound. *Extrinsic* laryngeal muscles anchor the larynx and assist the *intrinsic* muscles in bringing the vocal cords into the position most favorable for the production of the sound. It is with the action of these *extrinsic* muscles that we are here concerned.

Movements of the *extrinsic* laryngeal muscles are for the most part concealed from our view. Some observation, however, may be made of such action. If you look into a mirror and observe the back of your mouth at the instant that you commence to make a sound, you will observe a tensing of the muscles which form the rim of the soft palate.[6] The tension of these muscles will be noticeable at the sides of the *uvula* where they extend down the throat in the tonsil area. The arch will rise slightly and become narrower as the muscles contract (see Figure 18). The muscular tension at which you will be looking will be that of the *palatopharyngei* and *stylopharyngei* muscles. The contraction of these muscles is an instinctive part of tone production; it occurs as naturally and spontaneously as the contraction of muscles expelling the breath. As these palate muscles contract they pull upward on the rear horns of the *thyroid* cartilage to which their lowest fibers are attached (see Figure 19). When this action is opposed by a firm placement of the *hyoid* bone, it without question plays a role in the elongation and stretching of the vocal cords.

---

[6]If you are unable to see this movement while sounding an AH, it is because your tongue is in an unnaturally high position in your mouth. If that is the case, we hope that you will learn something from this chapter which will enable you to correct the fault.

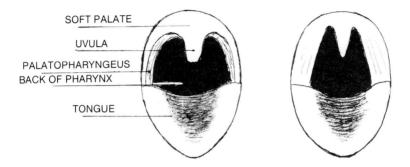

Figure 18. The illustration at right indicates the perceptible contraction of the *palatopharyngei* muscles (on each side of the uvula) when phonation takes place. The normal relaxed position, as in breathing, may be seen at left.

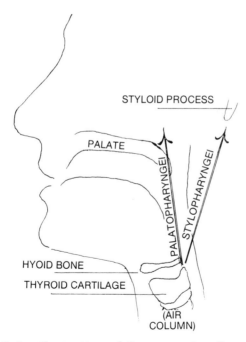

Figure 19. An illustration of the upward pull upon the rear horns of the *thryoid* cartilage when the *palatopharyngei* and *stylopharyngei* muscles contract.

193

Although the contraction of these muscles brings about a necessary function in the chain of coordinated actions involved in natural voice production, it may throw the vocal mechanism out of balance if other muscles fail to carry out their intended part of the natural coordination. To be more specific, if something does not counteract the lifting of the *thyroid* cartilage by the palate muscles, it will be pulled into an unnaturally high position. It may even be lifted so far away from its adjoining cartilage (the *cricoid*) that a complete collapse of sound may result. The inability of the vocal cords, held in an unnatural position, to restrain the force of breath would cause the tone to break.

It appears that a firm holding of the *hyoid* bone counteracts the upward pulling of the larynx when the voice is used correctly. This action, probably brought about through a contraction of the *hyoglossus* and *sternohyoideus* muscles, allows the *thyroid* cartilage to tilt forward on the *cricoid*, stretching the cords by means of the resulting leverage. Let us more specifically consider how this occurs.

It is the contraction of the *hyoglossus* muscle which draws the tongue into that grooved position so often associated with good voice production. One end of this muscle is attached to the underside of the back of the tongue, the other end is fastened to the rear horns of the *hyoid* bone (see Figure 17). If the muscle contracts, it pulls the rear horns of the *hyoid* upward. This brings about a tilting action of the *hyoid;* the front of the bone drops down and the rear horns rise (see Figure 20). The tilting action of the *hyoid* bone resembles the movement of an apothecary's scale; an upward movement at one end causes a downward movement at the other. If you

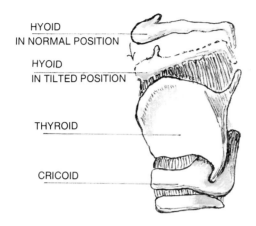

HYOID
IN NORMAL POSITION

HYOID
IN TILTED POSITION

THYROID

CRICOID

Figure 20. Showing the tilting of the *hyoid* bone when contraction of the *hyoglossus* muscle occurs.

possess the ability to draw the back of your tongue into a grooved position you can probably feel this action. Place the point of your index finger firmly on the front of the neck immediately above the *thyroid* cartilage, between it and the *hyoid* bone. Now while your finger still indents the neck at this point, make the groove in the back of the tongue. If you have made the groove correctly, by contracting the *hyoglossus* muscle, you will feel the front of the *hyoid* bone move firmly down to press upon the top of the *thyroid* cartilage.

Let us now consider the effect which this tilting action of the *hyoid* may have upon the stretching of the vocal cords. It has already been stated that the upward pull of the *palatopharyngei* and *stylopharyngei* can draw the larynx too far out of position unless something counteracts the upward movement. When the *hyoglossus* contracts, the *hyoid* bone is set firmly in position to block the

195

upward movement of the *thyroid* cartilage. The front of the cartilage moves slightly upward until it meets resistance from the front of the *hyoid* bone. When the resistance becomes great enough, the forepart of the *thyroid* cartilage is blocked in its upward movement (see Figure 21). However, the muscles which pull upward on this cartilage are attached to the rear of the *thyroid* (Figure 19) and, since the *hyoid* bone is raised in the back and attached by tendons to the back of the *thyroid* cartilage, the muscles are able to raise the back part of the *thyroid* cartilage. This brings about a tilted position of the *thyroid* which is similar to the tilted position of the *hyoid* (see Figure 21). The tilting action of the *thyroid*, which has been observed in the x-rays taken by Dr. Aatto Sonninen, is a slight one, but one which certainly has an effect upon the stretching of the vocal cords. Since the cords are attached to the front of the *thyroid* and rear of the *cricoid* cartilage it should not be difficult to understand how a leverage

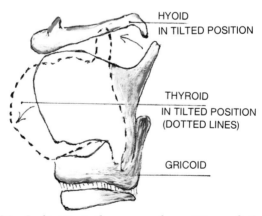

Figure 21. Indicating the normal position of the *thyroid* cartilage and its tilted position (dotted lines) caused by the upward pull of the *palatopharyngei* when the *hyoid* bone prevents the front part of the *thyroid* from rising.

action between the two cartilages may elongate the cords, hold them firmly in position, and stretch a larger part of their mass than might be done by the delicate muscles lying within the larynx. Perhaps an examination of Figure 22 may make this clearer.

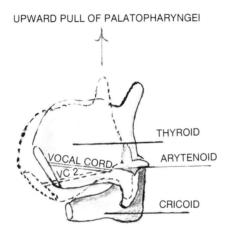

Figure 22. Illustrating how the vocal cords may be elongated by the leverage action between the *thyroid* and *cricoid* cartilage. Dotted lines show *thyroid* in tilted position. Dotted line marked VC² represents cords (at constant point of attachment to *arytenoid* cartilages which ride on *cricoid*) elongated by the tilting of the *thyroid*.

It should be reiterated that positive proof of such action as this must be established by scientific experiment. All that can be stated positively, at the present time, is that some few physicians[7] after careful investigation, believe that the extrinsic muscles of the larynx play a highly important function in stretching the vocal cords for singing; that

---

[7]Elmer L. Kenyon, "Extrinsic Laryngeal Musculature," *Arch. Otalaryngolica* June 1927, pp. 481-501.

x-rays taken by Dr. Sonninen prove that the *thyroid* cartilage moves forward and tilts on the *cricoid* cartilage when skilled singers are producing their high tones;[8] that there is a tendency for the larynx to move upward for high tones; and that common observation reveals that the back of the tongue is grooved when a baby cries, and either grooved at the back, or in a very low position when the best of singers produce "open" vowels.

An extensive and careful investigation of tongue positions by means of x-ray has been made by G. Oscar Russell.[9] However, the many x-rays taken by Dr. Russell were taken for the purpose of investigating vowel formation in speech and not for the specific purpose of investigating correctness of vocal production. The subjects of the investigation were not selected because of the excellence of their vocal quality, their exceptional power of voice, or the wideness of their vocal range. The photographs cannot therefore be taken as an illustration of what *should* happen in the correct production of tone but of what *does generally* happen in the formation of vowels.

Yet, there are several things about the remarkable photographs of Dr. Russell which are of particular interest in our present discussion of the importance of the tongue muscles in correct vocal production. The photographs make it apparent that

---

[8]Dr. Aatto A. Sonninen, "The Role of the External Laryngeal Muscles in Length-adjustment of the Vocal Cords in Singing," *Supplementum 130*, Acta-Otolaryngologica 3, (Stockholm 1956).

[9]G. Oscar Russell, *Speech and Voice*, (New York: The Macmillan Co., 1931).

many people produce tone while pulling the tongue back into the throat. This habit is more commonly observed when the person is making a vowel which is considered "dark" in quality; for example, an OO sound. The photographs clearly reveal that, although the forepart of the tongue may be raised to produce such a vowel as EE, the posterior portion of the tongue may be in a low position and that part extending into the throat may be pressed forward. Another interesting thing to be observed in the photographs is that the tongue is frequently grooved in that portion which is out of sight. Many of the photographs show that the sides of the tongue in the rear portion are in higher position than the center of the tongue. This means that, in these individuals, the *hyoglossus* muscle was contracted while the tone was being made. One other thing is of particular interest; the photographs show that while certain similarities of tongue position are associated with the pronunciation of specific vowels there are a variety of means of producing any one vowel.

This last observation is of interest because of the already expressed belief that the clear ringing tone which brings success to a singer **must** be produced with the posterior portion of the tongue pressed forward on every vowel that he sings (see Figure 23). If the throat portion of the tongue is consistently held in a position which may be described as forward, the vowels must be pronounced by alterations in the position of jaw, lips, visible portion of tongue, and vocal cord action. Scientific investigation does not refute the possibility of forming vowels through these means. For example, the OO vowel is usually made by pulling the tongue back into the throat (see Figure 24) and yet Figure

130 of "Speech and Voice" reproduces an x-ray taken of a child forming an OO with the posterior portion of the tongue pulled down, grooved, and thrust forward into a position similar to Figure 25. In commenting upon the photograph described above, Dr. Russell says, "Fig. 130 gives the u (OO) pronounced by a child who had still, at her early age, a distinctly unmodulated and anything but a 'soft-spoken' voice. Her voice had, rather, a piercing and barbaric quality (as children's voices tend to have before they are successfully softened by training). It will be noticed that the tongue arches well towards the front palate and takes such a position that the sound encounters no constriction between the soft surfaces of the throat, or otherwise until it reaches the lips."[10]

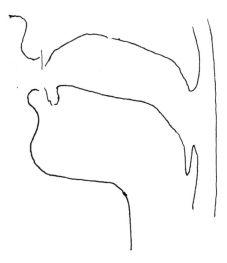

Figure 23. The tongue lowered in its posterior portion and lying forward in the mouth, a favorable position for singing.

---

[10]Russell, Op.cit., pp. 151-152.

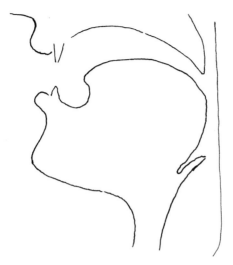

Figure 24. The tongue pulled back and raised in the posterior portion, an undesirable position for singing. This position is a frequently observed but unfavorable position for the OO vowel.

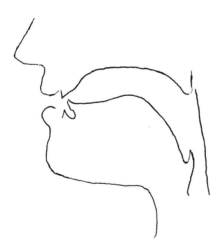

Figure 25. The tongue position of a young girl pronouncing an OO vowel. (After an x-ray photograph reproduced in Speech and Voice by J. Oscar Russell.)

These comments are highly interesting. Respectful of Dr. Russell's different purpose of study, I strongly suspect that this child emitted the natural kind of unrestricted tone which I feel is essential to the singer and to that person who would use his voice as it was intended to be used. This child, according to Dr. Russell, had anything but a "soft-spoken" voice. Is there a really great singer living who, at close range, has a "soft-spoken" voice? According to Dr. Russell this child had "a piercing quality (as children's voices tend to have before they are successfully softened by training)." Is such training successful? Are teachers who "modulate" the voice to "soft-spoken" not merely robbing the voice of its natural quality? Cannot the beautiful voice of that opera singer, who successfully projects his tone over a large symphony orchestra, be described in some degree as "piercing" when heard in close quarters, particularly so if the singer is singing a pitch similar to that of a child's voice?

It seems to the great singer that the throat does not change position while he sings; it **must** not change to any great degree. The human voice sustains a melody while forming various vowels. A basic tonal quality must persist throughout these vowel sounds if the singer is to achieve anything resembling the kind of sustained quality which we associate with the delivery of melodies by wind or stringed instruments. If the throat position (for the most part determined by the posterior portion of the tongue) is continually changing, there will be a resulting unevenness of sound. The tone will be altered by continuous changes in the size and shape of the throat, the most important of the vocal resonance chambers.[11] The tone will also be altered by the changing positions of the larynx and the varying degrees of firmness with which it is held in position. The singers efforts are hampered if the throat position is changed or the larynx moves from its normal position; vowels are formed with varying degrees of difficulty and each note of the scale seems to present its individual impediments. On the other hand, if the singer is able to retain the correct throat position, he will produce all the vowels, high and low tones, soft and loud tones without difficulty. He will have a feeling that the tone is a continuous thing; one that goes on without interruption as the fore-tongue, jaw, lips, seem to shape the words. He will always be prepared and able to take the high or low tones without readjustments. Acquisition of this correct position of the tongue (and its continuous application to singing) is necessary for the success of the singer. How can it be acquired?

The action of the tongue, correct or incorrect, is determined by the performer's auditory tonal image. If his mental concept of the kind of tonal quality which he should hear himself produce is incorrect, it will be reflected in a misbehaviour of the tongue. If his mind retains the sound and feeling which he has heard and felt when a tone was correctly produced and he strives to reproduce that sound and feeling, his tongue will assume the correct position. In other words, his tongue will assume the correct position if he is able to emit sound in an instinctive natural manner.

---

[11]Charles Frederick Lindsley, "Psycho-physical Determinants of the Individual Differences in Voice Quality," Psychological Bulletin, Vol. 30, p.594.

If the vocalist comes to understand the kind of brilliance and resonance which we hear in great singers, the tongue is much more apt to behave as it should. If he strives for mellowness of quality, the tongue is almost certain to be drawn back into the throat. In short, the proper brilliance, clarity, and carrying power in a voice go hand in hand with a posterior tongue position which may be described as down and forward. On the other hand, dullness of quality is concomitant with a tongue position that is raised and retracted.

We are unable to see the most important actions involved in singing. However, we are able to see half of the tongue if we look in a mirror. We, therefore, possess greater consciousness of the manipulations of the tongue than those parts of the vocal mechanism which are unseen. The back portion of that part of the tongue which is visible to us is so close to the realm of conscious control that the prospect of gaining mastery over its behaviour is a tantalizing thought to those who are aware of its importance. Perhaps someone will find a means of applying conscious tongue control in the teaching of singing. At the present time I have not found such a means and consider it more effective to approach the problem in an indirect manner.

Unless the student has acquired an incorrect behaviour of the tongue by long years of vocal misuse, I have found that the exercises given in this book gradually, or sometimes almost immediately, bring about the correct tongue position and some awareness of that position. The correction probably takes place in the following manner. The exercises are intended to reproduce sounds which are natural to a human being. If the student is successful in making the sounds, the tongue assumes its natural and proper position. After persistent repetition of successful efforts the singer commences to be aware of a throat position which he associates with those successful efforts. The singer's analysis of these physical feelings is not generally an accurate one but it is usually associated directly or indirectly with the tongue. He will find difficulty in describing the sensation, but will with vagueness usually refer to a feeling of openness at the back of the mouth, or to a raising of the soft palate, or less frequently to the tongue being pulled down and forward. Each of these sensations has been created by an action of the tongue, whether or not he realizes it.

An understanding of the tongue problem and its proper and improper behaviour in singing usually helps the student become aware of its correct functioning if the student is able, through the exercises, to bring it even occasionally to its proper action. Accurate diagrams, anatomical drawings, and pictures such as the x-ray photographs taken by Dr. Raoul Husson[12] of singers of the Paris Opera, are also helpful in giving the singer an understanding of the desired tongue position.

The singer is fortunate if the desirable behaviour can be brought about indirectly by the calling of tones. The movements of the tongue will then become a natural part of the complete vocal coordination. All possible effort should be made to bring about the correct position through this indirect approach before any unnatural method is attempted. However, there are those who have so misused

---

[12]Husson, *op.cit.*, pp. 12-15.

the voice that incorrect habits of the tongue stand in the way of all efforts to produce a correct tone. These people present a difficult problem which can only be approached through some direct physical means.

If, by some such means, the correct tongue position can be obtained, it is possible that even those whose tone is badly hampered by a misuse of the tongue can be led to make the correct tone. If the correct sound is brought about in this way, the singer or speaker may be assisted in the establishment of a proper concept, even though the approach has reversed the natural order of tone making. If the proper concept can be established, even by unnatural means, it may then come to be the naturally guiding directive of the voice.

I have found the inhaling sound (Exercises 2 and 2M) to be very useful in bringing forward that part of the tongue which is out of sight in the throat. If the vocalist is successful in making the sound, it is almost certain that the *hyoglossus* muscle is contracted and the throat portion of the tongue drawn forward to enlarge the pharyngeal opening. He may gain two valuable experiences through this. First, when this action occurs, it is usually retained for a few seconds during which tones may be emitted. The speaker or singer thereby gains a necessary experience of producing tones while the throat is in its proper position. Second, during the time that the tongue is being drawn forward and away from an obstructing position, it provides the producer of the tone with an opportunity to analyze the feelings associated with an open throat. However, even though I have found this exercise helpful in more than ninety percent of cases, it can fail. He who would develop his voice, perhaps with another's assistance, must judge whether or not it helps.

If all other efforts fail to reach the problem of an unruly tongue, then it would seem that some direct means of acquiring tongue control should be undertaken.

Learning to draw the back of the tongue into a grooved position should be the first step. This position is illustrated in Figure 26. If this exercise is performed as intended, the center line of the tongue, particularly at the back where the tongue goes into the throat, will be in a lower position than the sides of the tongue. It will result from pulling down the center line running from the front to the back. That back portion of the tongue which is normally visible when the mouth is open should be pulled down far enough to cause it to disappear from sight. To some this may seem a simple movement easily accomplished but to others it may, at first, seem an impossible maneuver. Any attempt to impose control of the tongue may cause it to stiffen, to rise, to do almost everything but that which is wished. However, with patience, it can be taught to assume the

Figure 26. Illustrations showing the tongue in a grooved position. This position results from a contraction of the *hyoglossus* muscle beneath the tongue. It is frequently to be seen in the mouths of great singers when they are producing tone.

207

sought after position.

In learning to silently groove the tongue, open the mouth and allow the tongue to relax in its normal position. If you are not then able to bring it into the grooved position by willful command, you may find it helpful to draw some object, such as a pencil, lightly along the center line. If the tongue remains somewhat relaxed, it will probably withdraw from the object at the place where it has been touched. The movements away from the object may, at first, be spasmodic but the skill can be acquired if the student is able to "get the feel" of that part of the tongue which should be drawn downward.

If one consciously contracts the muscle underlying the tongue and thereby pulls it into a grooved position, he is making a step toward conscious control of the *hyoglossus* muscle. However, it is but a simple step which must be repeated hundreds of times before anything that is helpful may result. If it is repeated many times, the student may come to understand a feeling of openness in the throat which he should associate with singing. This feeling of openness, which has previously been described, may feel like a raising of the soft palate rather than a lowering of the tongue. The open feeling may be described as an awareness of space between tongue and palate, of a kind of unhinged jaw position. The student may even have a feeling that the cheek bones are being raised or that he is at the beginning of a suppressed yawn. Such feelings as these, although they may only be associated illusions, can then be remembered and associated with further efforts to improve the tongue position while singing.

To repeat the exercise, simply allow the tongue to return to its normal position and to relax before again inducing the grooved position. Such practice should be done before a mirror until the student is absolutely certain that the tongue is actually doing that which he thinks it is doing.

Particular care should be taken to see that the larynx is not lowered while the tongue is being grooved. This can easily become an action associated with the grooving of the tongue but it need not be. It should be avoided. The voice will not function any better with a lowered larynx than with a larynx that is pulled high out of position. To make certain that the larynx is not being pulled below its normal position the student should place the thumb and index finger on each side of the front of the larynx, between the *thyroid* and *cricoid* cartilages. With the fingers in this position (see Figure 27) he should then make

PLACE FINGER HERE

Figure 27. Showing the point at which the right thumb should be placed in order to check on the stability of the larynx when the tongue is being grooved. The forefinger should be placed directly opposite the thumb on the other side of the larynx.

certain that the larynx is not lowered while the tongue is being grooved. If the exercise is performed correctly there will be no sense of strain or muscular exertion; the tongue will be contracted as easily as an eyelid is lowered.

After some proficiency has been gained in grooving the tongue at will, the student should try a variation of the same exercise. The tip of the tongue should be pushed forward, outside the mouth as far as possible. While the tongue is in this position it should then be grooved as deeply as possible. It is hoped that the back of the tongue will have dropped completely out of sight, giving the student the feeling that he has eliminated the right angle where mouth joins throat. There will be no inclination to lower the larynx while doing the exercise with the tongue protruded. If any actual attempts are later made to remedy a serious tongue fault by producing sound while intentionally holding the tongue grooved, the student and teacher must take care that the larynx is not lowered.

The complete vocal process is certainly too complicated to allow the singer to think of persistently holding a groove in his tongue while performing. It seems more likely that tongue grooving may be helpful if the student, while producing sound, will merely try to recall the feelings which he has associated with the grooving of the tongue.

Although, from my own experience, I cannot reccomend the conscious cultivation of a grooved tongue as the most propitious approach to learning to sing, I cannot dismiss the possibility that such an approach might be developed. I had personal acquaintance with two tenors who sang their ringing upper tones while the tongue was deeply grooved, and know from conversations with these two men that they were conscious of the tongue position and had been for many years. Each had originally gained conscious control of the tongue by doing "stunts" with it. Each had found personal amusement by grooving the tongue and had applied the skill sometime later to the production of sound. After successful attempts, they had associated the tongue grooving with correct tonal production and over a period of time had made habit of this tongue position while singing.

Every vocalist should have some knowledge of the importance of the tongue in singing and of the manner in which it should behave. Such knowledge may enable the speaker or singer to remedy his vocal faults and may give him part of that understanding of his own voice which he must have in order to continue to use it well. Such knowledge of the importance of the correct functioning of the tongue may enable him to analyze that aspect of his own voice production.

Certainly no harm can come from silent tongue exercises such as those described in this chapter. They probably offer the only hope to that person who misuses the tongue and cannot remedy the misuse by an indirect means. However, let me emphasize once again that, except in cases where bad habits are deeply established, it is very likely that the correct tongue position will be induced through the called sounds which have already been recommended. Producing sounds in this spontaneous way is instinctive to our nature. It is the direct means of bringing about the intricate coordination of actions which are demonstrated by great singers.

12

Who Should Teach Singing?

Titta Ruffo, one of the greatest of all baritones, was living almost penniless at the age of seventy-five on the top floor of a four story walk-up in Florence. The powerful voice, which at one time easily reached a sustained high C, had been practically gone for more than twenty years and the fortune that it had earned was also gone. At this time it was pointed out to him that there were many young Americans living in Florence who would be delighted to have an opportunity to study with the great Titta Ruffo and that their fees could provide him with a much needed living. "Why then," he was asked, "do you not teach?" The answer which he gave should be a monument to noble honesty. He said simply and directly, "I never knew how to sing, that is why my voice went by the time I was fifty. I have no right to capitalize on my former name and reputation and try to teach youngsters something I never knew how to do myself."

Unfortunately, very few who contemplate teaching seem to appraise their ability with the honesty of Titta Ruffo, nor do they face their responsibilities with any hesitation. Their complete disregard of the damage which may be wrought through poor instruction allows them to go blindly forth to destroy the hopes and ambitions of those who come under their guidance. Since no license is required and few established standards are set forth, the profession of vocal pedagogy includes many completely unqualified persons who cast a discrediting shadow upon those teachers who have spent years conscientiously studying the problems of singing and who have a background of knowledge and experience which should honor their profession. Those who are unqualified to give instruction in the use of the voice include natural singers, like Ruffo, who sang without knowing how; frustrated singers who failed in their own efforts and who have never been able to offer more than the instruction which brought failure to them; pianists, violinists, and conductors who have had no personal experience as singers, but who assume, because of their musical ability and some association with singers, that they are qualified to instruct in the use of the voice. In the realm of part-time instructors the list degrades the entire profession. Its quackery recalls the days when barbers served as physicians. Included in this list are, to my personal knowledge, a telephone repairman, an insurance salesman, an abundance of housewives who pick up a little extra money by teaching pupils in their neighborhood, a grocer, a drama director, and at least one judge!

Who is qualified to teach? What qualifications must a voice teacher have? The questions are difficult to answer because of the many aspects of singing. However, if a teacher makes any pretense at being able to develop voices, he can only be judged competent when his record proves that he has with consistency been able to bring fine quality, extensive range, power, freedom and ease of production to the voices of those who have come to him for help. If he limits himself to coaching (most coaches cannot refrain from meddling with voices), musicianship, knowledge of languages, knowledge of style, and general artistic background are essential qualifications. The ideal teacher of singing combines these qualifications with experience, a knowledge of the voice, and an ability to recognize correct tones.

It seems unthinkable that some voice teachers without singing experience themselves expect to improve the voices of others. It is difficult to imagine a successful ballet instructor whose training has been in playing the violin rather than dancing. It is unlikely that there are skiing instructors who have never been on skis or swimming instructors who could never swim. This first-hand experience with the subject gives an understanding of the problems, the sensitivity of the performer, and a recognition of correctness which cannot be obtained in any other way. It is not essential that the teacher's personal performances were highly successful; some of the best golf instructors have been players with limited ability. It is essential, however, that the teacher be sensitive to vocal faults, that he have understanding of the varied sensations which may be associated with correct and incorrect singing, and that he be able to help others in finding the correct manner of using the voice. His own vocal experiences, correct and incorrect, are invaluable to him in this objective.

It would be encouraging to aspiring vocalists if it could be said that the great voices of the world had been developed by singing teachers from the poorest voices. Unfortunately this has rarely been the case. There are those who had great natural voices before they went for their first lessons. There are those engaged in careers who feel a frightening insecurity in their positions because they know little of how they sing and fear to trust their voices to the guidance of teachers. There are those who through

215

some strange chance discovered their own voices; found them suddenly transformed from average to distinguished instruments which they then sought to cultivate. There have been very few noteworthy singers who began their study with really poor voices.

A more effective means of teaching singing is needed. Capable voice teachers have always been a rarity. If teachers of singing had consistently been able to develop great voices from average or below average talent, the biographies of successful singers would read differently. They would not indicate with startling consistency that those who achieved success possessed unusual vocal talent before they began to study.

It should be possible for almost any individual to develop a beautiful voice. It has often been thought that the great voice resulted from some unusual physical gift, but examinations have never proven that the vocal mechanism of the expert vocalist differed from that of the average singer. Most voice teachers, after a lifetime spent at teaching, have never been able justly to take credit for the development of one great voice. Many who have taken credit for the development of great singers have only given polish to the fine natural voices that came under their guidance. Even the famous singing masters of the seventeenth and eighteenth centuries cannot be given credit for having developed voices from the vocally handicapped or those who possessed average voices; only the most talented from a singing conscious Europe were accepted for training under their guidance.

A capable teacher is of great importance to an aspiring singer. Inability to hear the tone as others hear it and inability to view the action of the vocal mechanism give difficulty to the singer trying to improve his voice. These impediments, combined with psychological barriers and illogical reasoning, often lead the singer into a maze of confusion. Unfortunately for the person who needs help, the teaching of singing has usually been founded upon such unclear thinking that it has tended to increase, rather than eliminate, the misconceptions. There have been many teachers who have been able to differentiate between the desirable and the undesirable vocal quality, and these teachers have been of assistance to singers who were already capable of occasionally making a correct tone. However, the usual teacher has been of little assistance to people with mediocre voices, or to the skilled singer whose voice has been lost.

It is probable that more confusion and lack of agreement exists in the practices of vocal pedagogy than in any other teaching. There are those who base correct singing upon "correct breathing and diaphramatic support of the tone." There are those who emphasize "tone placement." There are those who hold to the traditional teaching of the so called age of *bel canto.* There are still others who would base correct singing upon the speaking voice, and there are countless other approaches, many of which are clothed in pseudoscientific expression which seems designed to attract the person who accepts our present age as one entirely of science.

Most teaching methods have evolved from the serious efforts of individuals to solve the problems which confront the teacher of singing. Nevertheless, there is much in teaching practices that is based on fallacious thinking. Some of the methods place emphasis upon a sensation which is actually the

217

result rather than the cause of correct vocal production and, in so doing, completely fail to strike at the basic problem.

It would seem wise to look backward to the teaching practices of that era referred to as the *bel canto* age of singing, if there was historical evidence to support the belief that the teaching methods were responsible for the great singing of that era. It is unquestionable that there were great singers during the seventeenth, eighteenth, and early nineteenth centuries. There are many interesting accounts concerning the singing that was heard from the stages of the opera houses during that period. In addition to the written accounts, there is the music itself which comes down to us as a testimonial of the skill of the most famous singers.[1] There can be no doubt that virtuosity in singing reached a level during this period that has probably never since been equalled. The teaching during this era certainly had a part in developing the astonishing ability for vocal display which brought acclaim to these singers. However, it may very well be questioned whether there were more great singers during any one generation of this period than at the present time and it may further be questioned whether the teaching was responsible for the development of the basic voices. The rewards for the successful singer were so great that thousands hoped for careers. Countless parents, seeing promise

---

[1]We cannot assume, however, that the operatic music written during the last half of the eighteenth century and first part of the nineteenth century was suitable for all operatic singers of the period, since the music was "custom made" for specific singers. Most of the operatic vocal music written before that time must be considered a bare indication of that which was performed. The manuscript only served as a springboard for the singer's dazzling improvisations.

in the voices of their sons, had the boys emasculated in the hope that they might become famous castrati. Countless numbers of parents guilty of thus depriving their sons of manhood lived to see disappointment in sons who were never able to fulfill their hopes. Dr. Burney, the famous eighteenth century British chronicler, wrote that in every town of Italy these pathetic figures could be found "without any voice at all, or at least without one sufficient to compensate for such a loss."[2] These aspiring singers must have had the desire to learn to sing, and surely they must have had some indication of talent. Yet, they failed! Would they have failed if the teachers of their time had really had any great understanding of the voice or a manner of developing it? One may search in vain through the writings of such famous teachers as Caccini, Zacconi, Cruger, Severi, Bacilly, Tosi, Mancini, for any real enlightenment as to how to develop a beautiful voice.[3] Their teaching, which

---

[2]Charles Burney, *The Present State of Music in France and Italy* (London: T. Becket, 1771) p.303.

[3]Giulio Caccini, *Le nuove musiche* (Roma: Raccolte Claudio Monteverdi [R. Mezzetti], 1930).

Ludovico Zacconi, *Prattica di musica utile e necessaria si al compositore si anco al cantare.*

Johann Cruger, *Preceptae musicae practicae figuralis,* 1625. Also in a German version, *Rechter Weg zur Singekunst,* 1660.

Francesco Severi, *Salmi passaggiati,* 1615.

Benigne de Bacilly, *Remarques curieuses sur l'art de bien chanter,* 1668.

Pietro Francesco Tosi, *Observations on the Florid Song* (London: J. Wilcox, 1742. Later English edition 1926).

Giambattista Mancini, *Practical Reflections on the Figurative Art of Singing,* translated by Pietro Buzzi (Boston: Gorham Press, 1912).

for the most part was devoted to the cultivation of vocal virtuosity, contains only the commonest generalizations and must have been largely based upon empirical practices. The *castrati* were given a thorough musical training in singing schools where they lived and studied for years. In these schools they received daily instruction and a training which produced great virtuosi. However, it must be remembered that technical display was the principal objective of the training and only the most talented and vocally gifted were admitted to the schools.

The person who looks at the melodies which Mozart wrote for his first love, Aloysia Weber, may marvel at the passages which soar upward to repeated F's above high C[4] and which contain skips as wide as two octaves and a third.[5] One might assume from this evidence of vocal prowess that Fräulein Weber was a product of great bel canto teaching, but Mozart gives us evidence to the contrary. Before she had had any formal training Mozart wrote, "she sings admirably and has a lovely, pure voice; she is fifteen. The only thing she lacks is dramatic action; were it nor for that, she might be the prima donna on any stage."[6]

The ambitions and the hopes of so many individuals are, and have been in the past, dependent upon the help which they might receive from vocal instructors. There are those individuals who find that an ineffective speaking voice is a handicap in

---

[4]e.g. The role of Vogelsang in *Der Schauspieldirektor*.

[5]e.g. Recitative and aria for soprano (K.418) *Vorrei spiegarvi, o Dio!, ah conte, partite.*

[6]Emily Anderson (ed.), *The Letters of Mozart and His Family* (London: Macmillan and Co., Limited, 1938), Vol. 2, p.661.

many aspects of life. There are others who desire to sing well as an avocation and emotional outlet. There are still others who lack the extraordinary voices which are so essential to them, if they are to fulfill their ambitions to have careers of acting or singing. Only a few of these people, who need great voices are actually being successful in developing them. Some study for years and end up with voices which are not basically improved. In many instances the voices, at the termination of their studies, are even worse then they were at the beginning.

I believe that teaching practices are at fault in many of these failures. I cannot accept most teaching practices of past eras because I find little in them that is worthy of perpetuation. I do not doubt that there were many good teachers in the past, nor do I wish to imply that there are no capable teachers at the present time. I do feel that effective vocal teachers are too scarce; that the thinking concerning vocal production has been, and generally is, very unclear and to a great extent erroneously founded. For this reason, it has been only the ingenious and highly talented teacher who has been successful and it has usually been only the naturally gifted vocalist who has fulfilled his ambition.

I have reexamined many teaching practices and expressions concerning the proper use of the voice. I have tried to accept only those practices or thoughts which seemed valid, and I have tried to add my own thinking to this, in the hope of presenting a more direct approach to the attainment of beautiful and expressive voices.

13

Technique and the Ultimate Goal

This has been a book of limited scope. It has not been intended as a comprehensive book on singing. Singing and speaking have many aspects. This has been a book limited to the development of a basic technique for producing the kind of tone which will expand the individual's ability to express himself through the voice. The student must never lose sight of the ultimate goal.

The painter learns to observe color and to mix paint. He learns the rules of perspective, he studies the bone and muscular structure of the human body, he learns to draw. These are techniques. If his desire is to be a true artist, he knows that these are *only* techniques which he is to use in expressing his observations of the world in which he lives.

The architect learns mathematics, drawing, engineering, and the qualities of available materials in order that he may bring reality to his visions.

The writer learns spelling and grammar. He develops his vocabulary and studies the means of effective expression in order that he may interest readers and more clearly express himself. He must have the technique for expression but that technique is only his to serve—he must have something to say.

And so it is with the person who would use his voice. The voice must be established. It must obey the command. It must serve for any expression which the mind dictates. It must convey the emotions and the intellectual nuances of the actor, the lecturer, the politician, the leader. It must serve the singer who more than any other faces the supreme challenges of vocal expression. He must have not only the ability to use his voice as a fine musical instrument, but also to convey through words and the music itself the broad arc of human feeling. He must recreate the expression of human emotion, the sensitivity to beauty, the delineation of musical patterns which were put into musical notation by the greatest creative musicians that this world has known.

Without technique the great latitude of vocal communication is not possible. Many talented and aspiring singers and actors experience handicap or total failure in their aspirations because of a basic lack of vocal ability. Many of those who would be spiritual, political, or business leaders fall short of their ambitions because of inadequacy of voice—the lack of a commanding vocal quality.

What is technique in the use of the voice? In piano, where the quality of the instrument is already determined, it implies learning to execute those functions necessary to transform the written music to pianistic sound, to develop virtuosity in the execution of octaves, scales, trills, thirds, sixths and so forth, as well as various kinds of "touch." Sometimes essentially the same kind of exercises have been used in an effort to establish a vocal technique. The practice of trills, scales, arpeggios and certain passages has also helped singers develop virtuosity, and it has contributed to the renown of those singers who interpret florid music. However, it has only given them great success if they also have great voices. It must not be forgotten that the training of a pianist and the training of a singer must be differentiated. With a pianist the instrument is there; he must only learn to play upon it. With the average singer the instrument must be built, it must be revealed and developed. Yet, even though the pianist must often accept the instrument which is at hand, he knows well that his performance will be hampered if the instrument is poor. If the choice is his to make, he does not select an instrument with weak tone, sluggish action, and poor quality. The singer is likewise limited if his voice is poor. Yet, unlike the pianist, it is within his power, if he is properly directed, to change, to enhance, to develop the instrument which is his.

In the establishment of a voice, first consideration must be given to the tone itself. There is individual quality in each voice but there are also distinctive characteristics which are common to all voices that function properly. Those characteristics are absent in the usual voice. The voice of the successful singer and that of the average singer stand in great contrast. Without the proper production of sound the vocalist is incapable of expressing the wide range and infinite shadings of emotions and feelings which the performer is called upon to express. If the voice is poorly produced it is without range and strength, and a person with such an instrument is unable to execute much of the great music which has been written for singers.

A proper manner of producing the tone must be established and it is to that aim that this book has been directed. It must be the first step in the development of an artist. Without it he will fail. The effort made in acquiring such a technique may require assiduous effort, it may be tedious in its routine, but it may also be fascinating in discovery, and exciting in achievement.

However, the vocalist must be warned that concentration upon the technique of tone production may cause the aspiring singer to lose sight of an artist's goal—a dedication to serve the composer in re-creating feelings which that composer could only convey by means of dots placed upon lines and spaces. The sensitivity to music, the ability to act through the voice, the presentation of the song, the delicate nuances, the dramatic declamation, the sincerity of emotional expression, all of the fine aspects of singing must be studied and cultivated. In these facets of singing, the singer may be assisted by the talented coach.

In conclusion, a relationship between the technique and the singer's loftiest goal must be pointed out. We began with observations concerning the influence of the human mind upon the voice. We must return to the mind in considering the complete expressiveness and the finesse with which an artist sings. A strategy, an overall plan, even detailed aspects of the interpretation of a song may be calculated and contrived. However, the greatest part of the expressiveness of a singing artist comes from the mind, from the sensitivity which one has developed through the experience of living, from a free flow of associations which are for the most part residing in the dark chambers of the subconscious. If the voice is produced as nature intended, that voice becomes the handmaiden of the mind, obeying the dictates of the master. The intangible inflections, the emotion which electrifies the tone itself, the elusive quality of a great artist are things that speak from the heart. The voice is a servant of our mentality. If the vocal production

is unnatural, the servant is bumbling, dull, ineffi-
cient and incapable of carrying out the wishes of the
master. If it is produced as God intended it, the
servant is faithful, efficient, and beautiful!

Concerning the Recording

Gratitude is expressed to the following singers for their recording of the vocal exercises.

Lucylle Anderson
Jean Doyon
Sharon Hofstedt
Lynne Hunnex
Douglas Caldart
William Lenard
Jeffrey Meyer
Jay Zorich

The excerpts from Shakespeare were read by the author who also recorded certain of the singing exercises.

ADDITIONAL COPIES OF THE RECORDING

For additional copies of the recorded cassette send $5 for each to Magnolia House Publishing, 2843 Thorndyke Avenue W., Seattle, Washington, 98199 U.S.A.

Typesetting and production under the direction of
Lauren Kurowski

Printed by
Litho Craft, Inc.
Seattle, Washington